TRUTH VS. TRADITION

HART, HOWARD

AUTHOR

"TRUTH VS. TRADITION"

TITLE

TRUTH

VS.

TRADITION

by

Howard Hart

**35707 N.W. Fairchild Drive
Woodland, WA 98674**

Po Box 192

Scriptural references in this volume are from the
Authorized King James Version. Where a variance from
the King James text is found, the translation or
paraphrase is my own.

Herald Publishing Company
P. O. Box 5646
Vancouver, WA 98668

Book and cover design and layout: Richard Mort
Printing and Binding: EMP Design, Printing & Publishing

Library of Congress Catalog Card Number 87-081508
ISBN 0-9618908-0-0

*"And ye shall know the truth,
and the truth shall make you free."*

– John 8:32 –

Table of Contents

CHAPTER 1

OLD NATURE, NEW NATURE
ONE NATURE, TWO NATURE 25

CHAPTER 9
TRADITIONAL RITUAL BAPTISMAL
REGENERATION

Introduction

I. The Power of Tradition.

A. The Cover

Tradition exerts a powerful influence over the truth. In the cover illustration the scales are tipped in favor of the weight of tradition. Truth should outweigh tradition and, in fact, tradition shouldn't really have an influence in the Christian realm, but it does. So, for this reason, I wanted to tip the balance of the scale back a little more to the truth. As you consider the weight of tradition in your own life as a Christian, I hope you also will have the desire to correct the imbalance of the weight of tradition as it affects your life. Do any of us really know how extensively tradition affects our lives as Christians?

B. "Three Measures of Meal."

Matthew 13:33 reads, "Another parable spake he unto them: the kingdom of heaven is like unto leaven which a woman took, and hid in three measures of meal, till the whole was leavened." If, as this parable has been interpreted, the three measures of meal represents "true doctrine", the leaven represents "corruption" and the woman represents religion in a bad sense, then the parable, no doubt, portrays the increasing pollution of true doctrine in

13

the "Kingdom of heaven." The pollution of true doctrine will ultimately result in a weakness of faith which produces an apostasy before the coming of the Lord. cf. II Thessalonians 2:3.

None of us, as Christians, want to be a part of the apostasy of which Paul speaks, but as we draw closer to the coming of the Lord we also are becoming more apostate because of doctrinal pollution.

The evidence of doctrinal pollution is almost overwhelming in these days. After viewing the "John Ankerberg Show" on television one is impressed with the great power of the doctrines of the cults to sway millions of souls from the true doctrine of Christ. We are thankful for this exposure of obvious doctrinal impurity. But what about the more subtle affect of doctrinal impurity in the parameters of evangelical, fundamental doctrine?

A missionary visiting the church I attend recently made a statement concerning the propensity for evangelical Bible preachers and teachers to accomodate one another in controversial doctrinal issues by "patting each other on the back."

It is my wish that this book may contribute to the exposure of traditional influence upon the true doctrines of scripture and that others will take up the responsibility of "speaking the truth in love."

C. The History of the Church and Tradition.

It is abundantly clear from history that tradition increases its influence over doctrinal purity in all ecclesiastical organizations. Even during the reformation denominations who have separated themselves from the tyranny of tradition are both incompletely separated from it and are continually being influenced by it. When the true church takes one step forward in doctrinal purity it ends up taking two steps back. Like one law of thermo-dynamics which teaches everything is "cooling down" and "slowing down", so, the "doctrine of Christ" is being swallowed up in tradition.

Not all is despair! God is still in control! His work is still getting done! Souls are still being saved, but there's a lot of faith being tarnished and a lot of joy being lost because of the overpowering influence of tradition.

II. The Dynamics of the Power of Tradition.

Why do we allow tradition to infiltrate the blessed doctrine of the Word? May I suggest two or three reasons that have occurred to me.

A. Scholasticism.

The "flesh" is subject to pride. All the world esteems a man of "letters" above his colleagues. I have watched as men have graduated from theological institutions after having served in fruitful ministries for apparently no other reason than to obtain recognition for their learning rather than their work.

Commentaries are written by "men of letters." To disagree with them in doctrinal issues is to challenge the letters behind their name. What happens to the doctrine and faith is of lesser value than a fellowship of "letters," so it seems.

That which is taught by biblical commentaries written by "men of letters" or "reputation" is then multiplied in institutions of theological training because of a loyalty to a seminary, a man of letters, or even a theological position. The students repeat and institutionalize the traditional concepts without questioning the validity of the source.

In reading an introduction to I John in a noted commentary the purpose for writing the book was eloquently described as a need to enhance fellowship among Christians, and to refute the Docetic and Gnostic heresies. This commentator included a list of his sources from which he, no doubt, produced his commentary. The most amazing thing is that both he and evidently his numerous sources failed to discover the reason for writing the epistle from the epistle itself. I John 5:13 gives the reason for writing. The epistle was written so that believers might know that they had received eternal life. In other words, the assurance of salvation is the central theme of the epistle of I John. There may well have been problems with heresy and Christian fellowship but they must be subordinated to the central theme of the epistle, the assurance of salvation. In my opinion, the misinterpretation of I John 1:9 in fundamental doctrine has been brought about by the failure to discover the purpose of the writing of the book. It seems too obvious to look within the book and discover the reason for writing but the "Wisdom of scholasticism" evidently barred that approach to interpretation.

B. Occupational Hazard.

By this title I mean the threat of losing one's job. A pastor is "called of God" but employed by his congregation. The congregation is much more difficult to deal with than God. Therefore, he must preach what the congregation expects to hear or he can be terminated. His paycheck comes from the congregation! Even if he has a congregation that is willing to accept truth over tradition, he has to preach doctrine that the fellow pastors in his denomination will accept or their opposition may result in his dismissal.

A tradition once established is a difficult doctrine to overcome. I have seen learned men in the Baptist denomination attempt to validate a plurality of leadership for Baptist Churches by the scripture (which I, also, believe is truth rather than tradition) overwhelmed by the numbers of Baptists who hold that leadership is vested in the pastor, alone, with the assistance of deacons. Because tradition has been established that Baptist Churches should be governed by a pastor or elder and deacons, more than one elder is not acceptable. It is interesting to note that at one time in the history of Baptist churches the plurality of leadership was "traditionalized" in "Baptist Confessions of Faith" 1646 number 36 and "The second confession" 1677 number 26.[1]

It would be very difficult for the president of a seminary, when discovering that the truth of scripture disagreed with the tradition of men, to espouse the truth if the tradition is well established in his denomination. To do so would be to lose his position as president of the seminary and his paycheck, as well. The sacrifice is too great, and one could rationalize that he could do better for the Lord by compromise rather than conflict. A teacher, as well, though he has a larger parameter of freedom for teaching truth vs. tradition must be careful not to interfere with well established traditions.

C. The Influence of the People.

Scholars, Presidents, Pastors, and Teachers aren't totally responsible for the influence of tradition as it obscures the truth of the Word. Christian congregations often would rather hear what appeals to the heart and mind rather than to face the truth of God openly. There is a strong tendency for those in teaching positions to approve that which the

---

[1] Henry Bettenson, *Documents of the Christian Church* (Oxford University Press, 1943), pp. 352-354.

people want to hear. II Timothy 4:3.

I was once asked to clarify my position on the salvation of infants by a couple in the church I pastored. I told them I knew of no scripture that guaranteed salvation of infants or children to a certain age which has often been called "the age of accountability." This means that up to a certain age children are held unaccountable for their sins and on this basis are guaranteed salvation. I believe there is a good scriptural answer for those that are concerned for the welfare and destiny of infants and children, but I wasn't allowed to give the explanation. They simply left the church without waiting for an explanation. Emotions run high on issues that personally affect us, and we opt for tradition if we suspect the truth might be too painful.

III. The Scope of Tradition.

A. A General Definition of Tradition.

Webster's Collegiate Dictionary, 5th Edition defines tradition as "Theol. a. Among Jews, an unwritten code of law given by God to Moses on Sinai. b. among Christians, that body of doctrine and discipline, or any article thereof, put forth or revealed by Christ or his apostles, and not committed to writing." The emphasis is the phrase "not committed to writing." That form of teaching which is extra-biblical. Teaching that has as its source information apart from the Holy Bible. "Apocryphal" or "legendary" teaching generally handed down by word of mouth and unauthentic is "traditional teaching." On the other hand, "truth" is general conformity to fact or reality.

B. The Antithesis of Tradition.

Biblically, Jesus Christ is the embodiment of truth (John 14:6). John 1:16 declares, "grace and truth" came by Jesus Christ. John 17:17 teaches that believers are "sanctified" by the truth and that God's Word is truth. Repeatedly, the scripture declares that God's Word is truth.

C. Warnings against Tradition.

There are numerous warnings for Christians to not turn from the truth of the Word of God. Jesus Christ rebuked the Pharisees for annulling the Word of God by their traditions. Mark 7:13. In Colossians 2:8 Paul warns Christians that they may be robbed of their faith by philosophy, deceit, and the tradition of men.

D. A Biblical Definition of Tradition.

Jesus Christ is the embodiment of the truth itself. The words that he spoke that have been recorded in the scriptures are truth (John 4:16; John 6:63; John 1:14, 17). Hebrews, chapter 2:1-4 warns Christians against turning from the truth "spoken by the Lord" and "confirmed unto us by them that heard them." A special endowment of miracles and gifts of the Holy Spirit proved the credibility of those who *heard* and relayed the words of Jesus Christ to us. The early church then cannonized the New Testament scriptures according to the "apostolic authority" of the writers of the New Testament. The Bible is a book of "truth" and not tradition. Tradition is extra-biblical material. Fundamental biblical Christianity accepts II Timothy 3:16 as a verification for the authority and veracity of the scriptures. On the basis of the extent and degree of God's participation in his written revelation we ascribe the word "inerrancy" to the context of scripture. Material that is in agreement with biblical truth is also "truth." Material that interpolates, supersedes, or contradicts biblical content is "tradition."

IV. The Necessity of Truth.

A. The Necessity of Truth for Faith.

Faith is believing! On the basis of credible evidence one may have faith. Faith affects the total person: his thinking, his emotions, and his expression of life. In Hebrews 11:7 Noah is a good example of one who has faith in God. God warned Noah of a coming flood. Noah's experience with God had taught him that God tells the truth, so he became emotionally motivated by the fear of the coming flood to make the expression of his life survival from the coming flood by the building of an ark. The degree of one's faith is in direct proportion to the expression of his lifestyle that is in agreement with the Word of God. The more traditional teaching he assimilates the less faith he expresses.

Romans 10:17 declares, in the context of preaching the Word of God, that "faith is from hearing and the hearing through Christ's Word. Faith is dependent upon God's word for spiritual rebirth, James 1:18; I Peter 1:23 and for the sanctification of life, John 17:17.

B. The Necessity of Truth for Interpretation.

Truth can only be interpreted by truth. Beyond the fact that only those who are the children of God by spiritual rebirth can understand the Word of God, (cf, I Corinthians 2:14) and that they require the Spirit of God to assist them in the understanding of the Word (cf. I Corinthians 2:12, John 16:13) is the clear teaching of Scripture that the Word of God is its own commentary on interpretation. That is, truth interprets truth. I Corinthians 2:13 tells us that the truth of Christian teaching is not dependent on human wisdom but on spiritual. the spiritual process of comparing spiritual things with spiritual things produces spiritual discernment. In II Peter 1:20 the apostle Peter warns us that a prophecy of scripture cannot be fully understood by itself. There is a mutual interdependency of truth for the understanding of truth. Presbyterianism, in 1643 by The Westminister Confession of Faith, declares concerning the Holy Scripture, "the infallible rule of interpretation of Scripture is the Scripture itself."[2]. The Second Baptist confession 1677 also included this statement.[3]

C. A word about Hermeneutics.

Hermeneutics is the science of interpretation. A great store of information is available to the serious student on the rules and principles of interpretation of the sacred text of scripture.

The elements of interpretation include such things as language, textual criticism, grammar and the historical influence on words, the scope and plan of a book as presented either directly or indirectly by the writer of the book, the context and the various influences that bear on the language of the text.

Though most writers agree that the science of hermen-

---

[2]Henry Bettenson, *Documents of the Christian Church*, (Oxford University Press, 1943), p. 347.

[3]Ibid, p. 353.

eutics may be divided into the elements of the grammatic-historical sense, the scope, context and plan, there is little effort made to prioritize the influence of any one of these elements over the others. In most cases the elements when used together produce a good literal sense of interpretation.

Because the Bible, itself, prioritizes one of these elements as exercising its influence over all other considerations I would like to make that emphasis, as well.

The context of scripture is by far the most important hermeneutical principle in the interpretation of scripture.

Although it is true that the Bible should be interpreted as any other book as far as language and grammar are concerned, it is also true that the Bible is not just "any other book." It has a divine author who has superintended its many co-authors in producing a non-contradictory revelation of himself and his people in history and the fulfilling of prophecy.

Time spent in word studies and grammatical distinctions are worthless if they disagree with the overall context of scripture. Studies made in the historical background and *usus loquendi* of words must be discarded if they disagree with the context of scripture. A thorough exegesis of a verse of scripture, it if disagrees with the overall context of scripture, must be regarded as a faulty interpretation.

Following the biblical line of reasoning then, it is extremely dangerous to make a doctrinal claim on a single verse of scripture. If a doctrinal distinction is made from the use of a single verse of scripture and it violates the context of scripture in any point it must be discarded in favor of the overall context.

The reason for making these several statements on the priority of context for interpretation is that, in my opinion, traditional doctrinal statements have been made from a single verse of scripture which violate the true context of scripture.

On the other hand, very positive doctrinal statements may be made when several verses find full agreement with each other and the overall context of scripture, concerning a spiritual truth.

It is also possible to become so engrossed in individual word studies that doctrinal assumptions may be brought forth that disagree with the context of scripture as a whole.

Since the author of the Bible is an infallible God, the context of a given word in sentence should agree with the sentence in which it is found. The sentence should be in agreement with the paragraph in which it is found. The paragraph should be in agreement with the book in which it is found. And the book should be in agreement with the Bible as a whole. The tests of cannonicity have deleted certain books as being part of the Holy Bible. The test of context should delete certain doctrines as traditional instead of truth.

In textual criticism we feel certain that we have perfected the sacred text of scripture by discarding any text found in a manuscript that is in disagreement with the majority of verifyable manuscripts. If we have relied so heavily on "context" for the perfecting of the New Testament text it seems logical to me that context should also verify doctrine.

It is with this approach to the interpretation of scripture that I have arrived at these several distinctions of "truth versus tradition."

You may be surprised, shocked, indignant and perhaps a little angry at the content of some of the chapters that refute a cherished or seemingly necessary tradition of faith. You may challenge the wisdom of attacking the "evangelical catechism." My motives are not to disrupt faith, but to strengthen it. Faith is not faith if it rests on extra-biblical information.

My experience has been that after the initial shock of being faced with truth, believers settle into a stronger, more peaceful and enjoyable Christian faith. There is a price to pay. The defenders of tradition are not afraid to attack and ridicule those who declare as Paul said, "Let God be true, but every man a liar." (Romans 3:4).

This book is not intended to be an exhaustive treatise on the traditions that devitalize the Christian faith. Neither do I suggest that the things I have written are irrefutable. I am subject to the flesh as are all Christians. However, following the testimony of the Scripture that the Bible is its own best commentary, I have discovered disagreement with some of the traditional teachings of evangelical theology. True faith is at stake! We ought to teach the truth!

I want to express my thanks to so many who have encouraged me to write this book. I am thankful for your prayers and for continuing to ask me, "How are you coming on your book." Here it is – May God's blessing be with you as you read it.

Chapter 1

Old Nature, New Nature, One Nature, Two Nature

*I*t has been taught in traditional evangelical theology that before spiritual rebirth takes place, we have an old Adamic unregenerate nature and that after spiritual rebirth takes place we acquire a new regenerate nature which dwells side by side with the old unregenerate nature. The result of this dual nature experience is a battle between the two natures with victory sometimes belonging to the new nature and sometimes to the old nature.

Because of the choice of the word, "nature" to define and compare human essence before and after spiritual rebirth a great amount of confusion has arisen and contradiction to the scriptural definitions of Christian essence. Theologians describe human essence as "old nature", "new nature", "Adamic nature", "old man and "new man." Some theologians suggest that even though a Christian possesses two natures they are not necessarily two personalities. It is also said that even though the old nature has been "positionally" put off, experientially the old man exists as an "active force" in the life of a Christian.

In defining the word, "nature" from the New Testament scripture it is discovered that eleven of the twelve occurrences of the word, "nature" are derived from the Greek word, "phusis" which means "growth by germination or expansion." It is further defined as "essence, native condition, birth, native species, kind, nature, natural frame, and native instinct." Webster's dictionary lists a definition for nature as "man's native, or original, state; the condition of simple, primitive man."

The word, "nature" as used in new Testament scripture includes both the body and spirit and must also include personality and its modification as a result of Adam's transgression. Man is by nature a personality. Personality modification occurred as a result of Adam's sin and personality creation also occurs at spiritual rebirth by the creation of new personality (IICorinthians 5:17) and the infusion of God's personality (IIPeter 1:4) within that new personality.

The concept of two personalities working in opposition to each other is contrary to the teaching of scripture. IICorinthians 5:17 declares, "So if anyone is in Christ, he is a new creation; the old things passed away, behold they have become new." The old personality has passed away; behold it has become new! Romans 6:6 also tells of the passing of the old personality in these words, "Knowing this, that our old man was crucified with him in order that the body of sin might be destroyed (or rendered useless) that we should no longer serve sin." In other words, the creation of a new personality brings about a curtailment of the practices of sinful flesh and ultimately a termination of sinful flesh by the resurrection to immortal, sinless flesh.

I. A diagram of a *traditional evangelical concept* of the nature of being before and after spiritual rebirth would look like this:

before rebirth – an unregenerate or Adamic nature dwells
in the body of flesh

after rebirth –   an unregenerate or
Adamic nature dwells
in the body of flesh   – positionally dead
– experientially
alive

plus:
– a regenerate nature dwells in the
body of flesh

A diagram of the *scriptural concept* of the nature of
being before and after spiritual rebirth would look like
this:

before rebirth – an unregenerate or Adamic nature
dwells in the body of sinful flesh

at rebirth   – the old or Adamic nature is terminated
Romans 6:6 in the body of sinful flesh

after rebirth – a new God-indwelt nature dwells in the
body of sinful flesh

II. The Old Man is Dead

As we consider the differences in the concept of being
before and after spiritual rebirth from the diagrams we note
that traditional theology teaches a continuance of the old
nature, or old man of which scripture teaches a termination.

Romans 6:6-8 makes it quite clear that a death has
occurred. Verse 6 says "our old man was crucified." As
with our Savior, the crucifixion that produced his physical
death is used to illustrate the death of the old personality.
Verse 7 tells us that the death of the old personality pro-

duces a freedom from sin. The Adamic nature is a sinful nature. Sin is intrinsically a part of the Adamic nature and no process of reformation is sufficient to remove the sin from the personality. Therefore, apart from reformation and by creation God produces a new personality to replace the old personality which has indwelt the body of sinful flesh from birth. A second birth is necessary to free an individual from sin. You must be "born again." John 3:3, 6, 7.

As Paul in Romans 7:1-4 uses the illustration of the death of her husband to terminate a marriage contract with him according to the law, so it is that God terminates the curse of sin by the death of the old man.

In Galatians 2:19-20 the apostle Paul describes his experience with the termination of the old man and the creation of the new as he says, "I have been co-crucified with – and I live no more." In this first expression of his new experience Paul makes it quite clear that he has experienced the death of the "old nature" or the "old I." He then continues by saying "but Christ lives in me." Even though there has been a death he still retains personality for he says, "Christ lives in *me*." A new personality has arisen at spiritual rebirth. The old has gone and a new personality stands in its place. Paul then describes the new experience of a God indwelt personality in these words, "and what I now live in the flesh I live by the faith of the Son of God." That is, my new life experience is one that I am constantly sharing with the Son of God. This is the normal productive Christian experience! He completes the sentence by reminding himself that the one with whom he is sharing life is the One who is still loving and giving himself for Paul.

Another verse which teaches the death of the "old man" is Ephesians 2:3. In Ephesians 2:1-10 Paul is describing the change that takes place as a result of spiritual rebirth. In verses 1-3 he gives a description of the unregenerate state. In verses 4-9 he tells us how regeneration happens. Then, in verse 10 he tells us of the results of regeneration. "We are a product created in Christ Jesus." This new created product is a new man, a new personality, alive in the person of Jesus Christ. The result of creation and infusion in Christ's personality is that we produce good works that God has planned for us to perform. Good works are the result of the creative design of God. It's really all we are capable of producing from the new man.

But the word that is really important to impress us that the old man is dead is the word, "nature" found in verse three. Paul says you "*were* by nature the children of wrath." In other words, you *were* by *essence* or *nature of being* children of wrath. But now, you are not the old beings that you were because your old man has been crucified and no longer exists. We simply cannot accept the concept of the continuation of the old nature when the scripture teaches us in the very word we are using that it has ceased to exist because we have been created by God's grace in Christ Jesus unto good works.

A fourth scriptural point that must be answered by those who believe the old man is alive as an "active force" in the Christian life is why the old man or the influence of the old man is not mentioned in passages that specifically speak of the battle that exists in the essence of Christian being. In Galatians 5:16 the two elements of Christian essence are spirit and flesh. There is no mention of the "active force" of the old man as a second opposing influence on the spirit. In verse 17 the opposing influence of the flesh is repeated two more times and again without reference to the old man's influence.

In Romans 8:10 the essence of being is described as a dead body and a living spirit with no mention of an old man. In Colossians 3:3 which is in keeping with Romans 8:10 the essence of being is described as both dead and living with

Christ in God. The argument of silence on a doctrinal issue is perhaps not as conclusive as objective truth yet if the doctrine of the continuation of the old man is a part of New Testament truth one would expect to find some indication of it somewhere. When Paul describes specifically the essence of Christian being in I Thessalonians 5:23 as being spirit, soul and body he makes no mention of the Adamic nature.

III. We Are Dead To Sin

Traditional evangelical theology teaches that "even though we are dead to sin, sin is not dead to us." This sort of double talk concerning sin is similar to the "positional" death and "experiential" life of the old man. According to this teaching, the Christian is locked in a continual battle with both the old man and sin. Actually, the scripture teaches that the Christian is *dead to both.*

In Romans 6:2 Paul asks the question, "How shall we who died to sin yet live in it?" This verse does not say we are dying to sin but that *we died to sin,* and not that we are dead to sin but that *we died to sin.* This is a completed transaction that occurred in our past experience. Thus, sin is no longer a part of our life!

Immediately, I can hear the question, "If sin is no longer a part of my life then why do we sin as a Christian?" The answer is that you *as a Christian* don't sin! That part of your essential being that is *in Christ,* the sinless one, cannot and will not, bring sin into the person of Christ. The part of you that is in Christ is spiritual. This is the real you, the eternal you. The body that you live in, the brain that you think with, and the emotions of a physical nature are your flesh and this part of you, while you are alive in the body *always* has sin dwelling in it! But the flesh is not the real you! It is that which is mortal and will pass away. The flesh is the vehicle through which one expresses spiritual life on earth. When you die or are raptured the real you will go into the presence of the Lord. To those who die before the rapture their real person will go into the presence of the Lord in an immortal spiritual essence, only. IICorinthians 5:8. Those who are raptured will go into the presence of the Lord in a spiritual and physical immortal essence. At the time of the rapture those who have been experiencing a spiritual presence with the Lord will also receive the additional physical essence. I Thessalonians 4:13-18.

Romans 7 is the best scripture for discerning between the spiritually sinless essence and the physical sinful essence called "flesh." The identification of the word, "I" in the passage of scripture from verse 15 to verse 25 reveals two types of awareness that a Christian experiences as a "new creation" in the flesh. At times Paul responds from a spiritual awareness separate from the flesh and at other times he responds from a spirit and flesh awareness. However, he never loses sight of the true separation of the spirit and the flesh. An exercise of identification of awareness from the word, "I" and "me" in this passage from the King James version would be as follows:

verse 15 – 1st "I" the spirit and flesh awareness
      2nd "I" the spirit awareness
      3rd "I" the spirit awareness
      4th "I" the spirit and flesh awareness
      5th "I" the spirit awareness
      6th "I" the spirit and flesh awareness

verse 16 – 1st "I" the spirit and flesh awareness
      2nd "I" the spirit awareness
      3rd "I" the spirit awareness

verse 17 – 1st "I" the spirit awareness
      1st "me" the spirit and flesh awareness

In this verse Paul recognizes that sin is not being generated from the new man or the new creation but from the flesh in which it resides.

verse 18 – 1st "I" the spiritual awareness
1st "me" the spirit and flesh awareness

At this point Paul clearly identifies the source of sin as being in his flesh as he says, "For I know in me (*that is in my flesh*) dwelleth no good thing."

2nd "me" spiritual awareness
2nd "I" spiritual awareness

verse 19 – 1st "I" spirit awareness
2nd "I" spirit and flesh awareness
3rd "I" spirit awareness
4th "I" spirit and flesh awareness

verse 20 – 1st "I" spirit and flesh awareness
2nd "I" spirit awareness
3rd "I" spirit awareness
1st "me" spirit and flesh awareness

Now for the third time Paul is making it clear that his new man is not sinning but that the source of the expression of sin is the flesh.

verse 21 – 1st "I" spirit awareness
2nd "I" spirit awareness
1st "me" spirit and flesh awareness

verse 22 – 1st "I" spirit awareness
1st "inward man" spirit awareness

verse 23 – 1st "I" spirit awareness
1st "me" spirit and flesh awareness

verse 24 – 1st "I" spirit and flesh awareness
1st "me" spirit awareness

verse 25 – 1st "I" spirit awareness
2nd "I" spirit awareness

It is easy to discover from this passage the complete separation of the spirit and flesh and also the hindering affect of the flesh on the spirits' liberty in Christ. Paul's summarization of this hindering affect of the flesh in verse 24, "O wretched man that I am! Who shall deliver me from the body of this death?" leaves no doubt in the mind that the imprisonment of the Spirit in the body of flesh is an unhappy experience for him. Also, in verse 25, he describes an experience in which he can never gain a 100% victory in spiritual expression.

It is possible for a Christian to say, "I have no sin and I commit no sin" when he is speaking of his true spiritual essence, alone. It is also possible for a Christian to say, "I am continually sinning and always have sin in me" when he is speaking his true spiritual essence captive in the body of sinful flesh. Both statements are truthful and accurate but they depend on the point of awareness from which they are spoken to be true.

In the book of 1st John in which the apostle is, according to I John 5:13, revealing evidence so that a true believer may know he possesses eternal life both antithetical statements are found concerning sin and both are true! In I John 1:8 a solid evidence of salvation is that one must agree that *"has sin"* and in verse 10 that he *"has sinned."* To deny that sin reposes in the Christian life or that sin is not expressed by the Christian life is a lie and those who deny the basic truth concerning sin are not honest and are not really saved. From the spirit plus the flesh awareness this is a true statement.

However, it is also possible to speak of the spirit essence only and make statements about its sinlessness. I John 3:8 and 9 the antithetical statement about the sinlessness of the new man in Christ is given as John says, "the one doing sin is of the devil, because the devil sins from the beginning." In other words, those who sin are following the characteristics of the devil, their father. (cf. John 8:44). This preface to the 9th verse has caused some commentators and even translators to interpret verse 9 to say that "whoever is born of God does not *practice* sin." However, the word, practice, does not occur in this verse and the statement made by John the apostle agrees with that of Paul when he says, "everyone born of God *does not* sin because his seed remains in him; and he *cannot sin* because he has been begotten by God." (cf. Romans 7:17, 18, 20).

That part of us that is born of God is a new creation, a sinless creation and is incapable of sinning because it doesn't have the power to sin according to John the Apostle.

Therefore, as long as we are able to walk in spirit awareness, we are unable to fulfill the lust of the flesh. (cf. Galations 5:16). When our center of awareness slips into the flesh, carnality, as Paul calls it in I Corinthians 3:3, takes over and we in a spirit-flesh awareness fulfill the lust of the flesh. (Please see the illustrations of human essence before and after salvation to better understand the dynamics of committing sin by a Christian, pages 35-38.)

IV. The Hindrance of the Flesh

There is never a time, as long as a Christian dwells in mortal flesh, that he is not hindered in spiritual achievement. He will never be 100% able to fulfill the desires of the spirit. It must also be said that the flesh will never have a 100% dominance over the Christian as it had before conversion. Continuation in carnality for an extended period of time, depending on circumstances, may result in the chastening of the Lord. (cf. Matthew 18:15-19, I Corinthians 5:5, I Corinthians 11:30, Hebrews 12:5-8, James 5:15, I John 5:16).

An Illustration of Human Essence Before Spiritual Rebirth

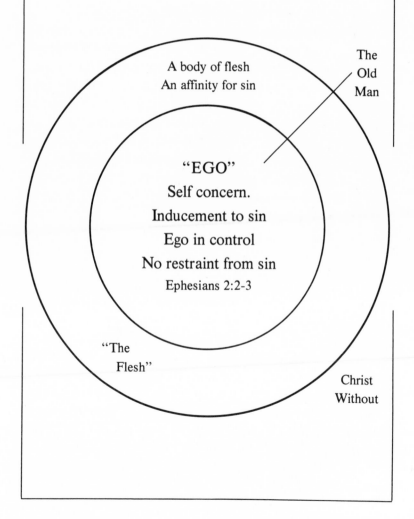

A body of flesh
An affinity for sin

The
Old
Man

"EGO"
Self concern.
Inducement to sin
Ego in control
No restraint from sin
Ephesians 2:2-3

"The
Flesh"

Christ
Without

An Illustration of Human Essence After Spiritual Rebirth

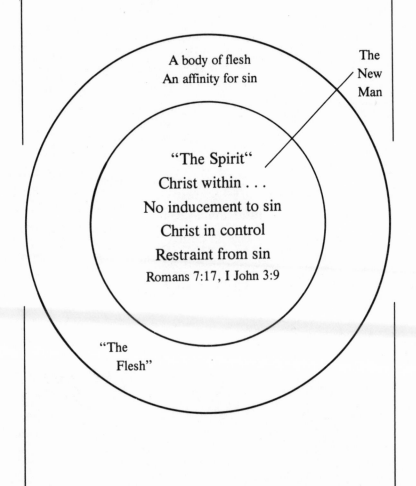

A body of flesh
An affinity for sin

The
New
Man

"The Spirit"
Christ within . . .
No inducement to sin
Christ in control
Restraint from sin
Romans 7:17, I John 3:9

"The
Flesh"

An Illustration of Human Essence While Walking in the Spirit

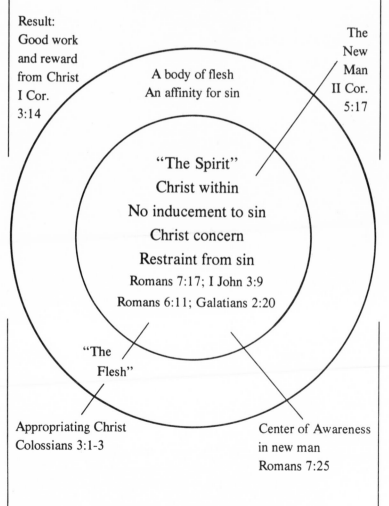

Result: Good work and reward from Christ I Cor. 3:14

The New Man II Cor. 5:17

A body of flesh
An affinity for sin

"The Spirit"
Christ within
No inducement to sin
Christ concern
Restraint from sin
Romans 7:17; I John 3:9
Romans 6:11; Galatians 2:20

"The Flesh"

Appropriating Christ
Colossians 3:1-3

Center of Awareness
in new man
Romans 7:25

An Illustration of Human Essence While Fulfilling the Lust of the Flesh

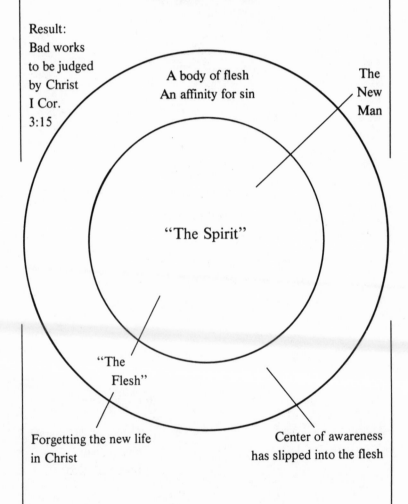

Result:
Bad works
to be judged
by Christ
I Cor.
3:15

A body of flesh
An affinity for sin

The
New
Man

"The Spirit"

"The
Flesh"

Forgetting the new life
in Christ

Center of awareness
has slipped into the flesh

The question in Romans 6:2, "How shall we who *died* to sin yet live in it?" is answered by a resounding, "We shall never live in sin again." Why is this so? Because we are forever separated by Christ's death, burial and resurrection from sin. Sin is not in our new man and our new man is separated from the flesh through *a new creation in Christ.*

When sin appears in a Christian life its source and expression comes through the flesh, not the spirit. The new man can neither generate nor express sin. The new man is not responsible for sin! What a liberating concept this is for the one who loves the Lord. His love is faithful and true, he's really not double minded. The weakness that allows the expression of sin from his life is not a character weakness but a lack of maturity in learning to appropriate the presence and power of Christ to overcome the aggressive magnetism of the flesh to sin and its expression.

The Christian life is an unequal yoke of a sinless new man in Christ with a sinful flesh. It is unequal because the new man desires to fulfill righteousness, the law of God, but the flesh lusts to sin. The spirit is immortal but the flesh in temporal. The spirit possesses divine personality but the flesh possesses irrational sentient animalism.

The exercise of sin in the Christian life is both originated and exercised through the flesh. One might conclude, then, that since the new man is not repsonsible for the sin, a Christian is free to sin as much as his flesh desires. Although the Christian is not directly responsible for the expression of sin he is responsible to control the flesh. Galatians 5:16. He must not present the members of his body as instruments of unrighteousness to sin. Romans 6:13.

We must mortify the deeds of the body. Romans 8:13. We must *put on the Lord Jesus Christ* and make no plans for the lust of the flesh. Romans 13:14. We are not told in scripture to make war with sin but to control the flesh in which sin resides. The result will be the curtailment of sin as an expression from the Christian's life.

Having died to sin (Romans 6:2) has several blessed concepts.

1. I am separated from sin because it is not a part of me; It resides in my flesh. Romans 7:17, 18, 20.

2. I am separated from sin and, with Christ helping me, I'm able to control it's expression by controlling the flesh which is the vehicle of its expression. Galations 2:20.

3. Jesus Christ is constantly and faithfully cleansing sin in the flesh, Romans 8:3, I Peter 1:2, I John 1:7, so that I have a clean vessel or vehicle for the expression of the life of the new man.

4. The control of sin in the flesh should become easier as I mature in Christ through transformation by the renewing of the mind, Romans 12:2, II Corinthians 3:18.

V. Concluding throughts on the Old Nature and New Nature.

Spiritual rebirth which is the creation of the new man in Christ results in a complete change. As II Corinthians 5:17 tells us all things become new. We have a new personality. We have a new relationship with Christ. We are blessed in a new covenant with God in which he writes His laws in our mind and heart so that we are motivated by knowledge and desire to obey him. In the new covenant we are guaranteed the forgiveness of sin in a cleansing so complete that our God promises to never remember our sins again! (cf. Hebrews 8:10-13, Hebrews 10:14-22). We died to sin and it no longer has any jurisdiction over our lives,

Romans 6:2. We have also died to the law as an external influence over our life. Romans 7:4. We now obey God because we want to rather than because we must obey. All of the written ordinances with their details were nailed to His cross, Colossians 2:14-17, so that we breathe the fresh air of a new covenant in a new freedom and a loving personal relationship with God.

How disappointing, then, to have a traditional theology resurrect an old man to haunt us and dig up the sin that has been forgotten to depress us when Christ died to set us free! John 8:32.

VI. Scriptural Summary of the Identity and Sanctification of the New Man.

The Identity of the New Man.

The new man is a sinless new creation of personality dwelling in and indwelt by Christ that inhabits a body of sinful flesh.

A. Creation of new man.

Romans 6:6 – "our old man was crucified"

IICorinthians 5:17 – "a new creation" "in Christ" cf. Galatians 6:15

Galations 2:20 – "Christ liveth in me"

Ephesians 2:10 – "created in Christ Jesus"

Ephesians 4:24 – "created in righteousness and true holiness"

Colossians 3:10 – "renewed in knowledge after the image of him that created him"

II Peter 1:4 – "that by these ye might be partakers of the divine nature"

I John 3:9 – "everyone having been begotten of God does not sin because his seed remains in him and he cannot sin because he has been begotten of God"

Romans 6:2 – "we who died to sin, how shall we yet live in it?"

Romans 7:17 – "I no longer work it but the indwelling sin in me"

Romans 7:18 – "I know that in me (that is, in my flesh) dwelleth no good thing"

Romans 7:20 – "It is no more I that do it but sin that dwelleth in me"

Romans 7:25 – "with the mind I serve the law of God but with the flesh the law of sin."

Colossians 3:3 – "you died and your life has been hidden with Christ in God"

II Timothy 2:11 – "If we died with him, we shall live with him"

B. Sin and new man.

John 1:7 – "the blood of Jesus Christ his Son cleanses us from all sin"

I Peter 1:2 – "Elect – unto obedience and the sprinkling of the blood of Jesus Christ"

I John 2:2 – "he is the propitiation for our sins"

Romans 8:3 – "condemned sin in the flesh"

Romans 6:2 – "we who died to sin"

Hebrews 10:17, Hebrews 8:12 – "their sins and their iniquities will I remember no more"

Romans 6:7 – "he that is dead is freed from sin"

Romans 6:11 – "reckon yourselves, to be dead indeed to sin"

I Peter 2:24 – "we being dead to sins"

C. Sanctification of the new man.

Romans 12:2 – "be ye transformed by the renewing of your mind"

Ephesians 4:22-23 – "that you put off as regards your former conduct" and "be renewed in the spirit of your mind"

Colossians 3:10 – "being renewed in full knowledge according to the image of the one creating him"

Ephesians 4:24 – "put on the new man created in righteousness and true holiness"

Romans 6:11 – "reckon yourselves to be dead indeed unto sin but living to God in Christ Jesus"

II Corinthians 3:18 – "beholding (in a mirror) the glory of the Lord are being changed into the same image" James 1:25

John 17:17 – "sanctify them through the truth"

John 15:4 – "abide in me"

Ephesians 5:26 – "that he might sanctify and cleanse it with the washing of water by the word"

Galatians 5:16 – "walk in spirit and lust of the flesh you will by no means perform"

Romans 8:13 – "if by the Spirit the practices of the body you put to death you will live"

Romans 13:14 – "put on the Lord Jesus Christ and make no forethought for the lusts of the flesh"

Romans 6:13 – "neither present your members as instruments of unrighteousness to sin but present yourselves to God as *alive from the dead* and your members as instruments of righteousness"

VII. Questions Concerning the Two Nature Concept of Christian Essence.

A. What happens to the old nature at death? If the old nature and the new nature indwell the body of flesh during a Christian's life the question as to the destiny of the old nature must be asked. There is a clear teaching in scriptures that the "new man or the inward man" goes into the presence of the Lord at the death of the physical body. cf. II Corinthians 5:6-8. It is also quite clear from scripture that the "old man" or "old nature" in the case of the unregenerate goes to hell and suffering when physical death occurs. cf. Luke 16:22-23.

Does the old man or old nature go to hell as in the case of the unregenerate? There is no scripture that teaches of such a destiny for a Christian's "old man." Does "he" just cease to exist at physical death? Is there a place in heaven for the "old man" and does a Christian forever subsist in a dual personality? If the old man is not a personality as is implied by the equation of terms, "old man" and "new man" or "old nature" and "new nature" then what is he? If he is a part of "flesh" or a part of the "body of sin" then why give special recognition to him? The scripture gives no such recognition to an "old man" or "old nature" after spiritual rebirth. The two terms "spirit" and "flesh" or "outward man" and "inward man" the mortal and immortal are the two parts of Christian essence after regeneration.

Romans 6:6 teaches that the "old man" has been crucified with Christ. Since the flesh continues as a vehicle to house the spirit and remains until physical death the "old man" cannot be a part of the flesh. Conversion is more than the reformation of the "old man" by an indwelling presence of a "new man." It is, in fact, the termination of the "old man" and the creation of a "new man" in Christ Jesus.

B. Assuming that the "old man" continues in the life of a Christian what relationship does the Christian sustain towards him? We are told that we must control the deeds of the old man by fellowship with Christ, the power of the spirit and with the word of God. We must now regard all that we have experienced in the past in the complexity of human experience as our enemy. We must make our new man stronger so that "he" can control the "old man." We must make a vital part of our life inoperative. We must sever the fondness for him and try to forget the memories of life with him alone in favor or the "new man" who has now come into our lives to take control and lead us to the "holy walk" with the Lord. "He" will try to assert himself and reestablish his expression of life through us but we must not let "him." We must try to extinguish "his" life although we will never be completely successful. Such teaching as this demoralizes the Christian with a mixed sense of loyalty to his dual self and is not a part of the teaching of scripture. It is in fact traditional! It, no doubt, orginated by some well-meaning person trying to analyze and describe the conflict he was experiencing in his Christian life. Romans 6:5 says, "we have been planted together in the likeness of his death." We must leave the "old man" buried. Romans 6:6 says, "Our old man has been crucified with him," so let's not try yo revive the crucified, dead "old man." Let's believe scripture that teaches "if we walk in the spirit we shall not fulfill the list of the flesh." Galatians 5:16. Our fellowship with Christ in the "new man" is not one of fighting sin and the flesh but of walking in the spirit with Christ. That's positive! That's liberating!

C. How can all things be new as II Corinthians 5:17 teaches if we still retain an "old nature" or an "old man?"

Some would perhaps seek to answer a question like this with the question: "How can all things be new if we still live in an "old body of flesh," in the same "old world" and in the same "old daily grind?" If we still retain the "old nature" or the "old man" as a part of our spiritual being then this verse isn't true. If, however, as scripture teaches, we are "born again" made a "new creature" and if all of us that is spiritually immortal is a new creation, then because we are a new creation, a new man, we sustain a new relationship to an old environment. We see through the "spiritual eyes" of the new man and relate to the "old body of flesh," "the old world" and the same "old daily grind" from a new center of being. As a new man in Christ we have an entirely new attitude and experience with the "old things" of this world. It would not be possible for us to have these new experiences and attitudes if we still possessed the "old nature" or the "old man." If "he" existed "he" would inject old attitudes and experiences into our life with Christ. In Galatians 2:20 Paul tells us he has been "crucified with Christ" and that he no longer lives. This makes sense because crucifixion produces death. Then, he says, "But Christ lives in me and my life in flesh is lived by the faith of the Son of God." In other words, I now possess a new life by faith and in fellowship with Christ. His old man is dead; his new life is in Christ; all things are new!

In John 12:24 and 25 Jesus Christ makes it quite clear that new life cannot come forth unless there is the death of the old. The old grain of wheat must die! And, if it dies, it brings forth much fruit. Salvation and eternal life can occur *only* if there is a death of the old life. cf. verse 25.

It is dangerous theology of salvation to hang on to a tradition of the continuance of the old man when both Christ and Paul teach that *all* things must be made new through death. Even the body of flesh must be made new at the resurrection.

VIII. The Blessings of the Scriptural Concept of Christian Essence.

A. The Christian experiences a new freedom from sin as he discovers the true essence of his being!

The two nature concept of sin teaches that sin is generated in the "old nature" or the "old man" and since the "new man" isn't strong enough to control the "old man" the "new man" sins because of the coercion of the "old man." Thus, the struggling Christian is under the guilt of his sin as a new creation and depending on his attitude toward the "old man" may experience some guilt for the deeds of the old man or at least for not controlling the influence of the old man. To solve the problem of the guilt of sin I John 1:9 is pulled from its context and now becomes a source of help to remove the guilt that this teaching places on the mind and heart of its followers.

An explanation of the misinterpretation of I John 1:9 because of traditional teaching is included in this book under the chapter title, "The Unconditional Cleansing of Sin." Please refer to this chapter for an explanation of the traditional and scriptural teaching of this verse.

Beyond the fact that I John 1:9 is not teaching a method of cleansing of sin for the Christian is the solid scriptural teaching that a Christian is dead to sin. Romans 6:2 says so! Then, Romans 6:7 tells us that he that is dead is "freed from sin!" How is this possible? The old man had a sin nature! The old man was sinful! The description of his sinfulness and his motivation to sin is described in Ephesians 2:2-3. We were motivated to sin by satan "the prince of the power of the air." We had a spirit of disobedience. We fulfilled the desires of the "flesh" and of the "mind." We were naturally, intrinsically, sinners and we faithfully sinned according to our nature. But the old man that we were is crucified! He's dead and buried and with him, his nature.

There is a new man in his place, a new spirit-being indwelling a body of flesh. The new man is dead to sin because (1) sin is not in him (2) he is not in sin but in Christ. He is a new creation created for good works and not for sin. Ephesians 2:10. He is born of God and *cannot* sin because of God's seed in him. I John 3:9. Think of that! A Christian was never designed to sin and cannot sin and is dead to sin! That's *real freedom* from sin! There is sin in the flesh and it's always there, but it's not a part of me. My flesh is not the real me. I'm completely separate from the flesh. It's only the vehicle in which I am imprisoned until death or the rapture. And then, I am totally free from it. When I'm not walking in spirit the flesh may exercise or express the sin that constantly resides there. But when I walk in the spirit; in awareness of Christ's presence and power the flesh is controlled and cannot fulfill its lusts. Galatians 5:16.

As a new man, a new creation in Christ, I have no sin in me (i.e. in my spiritual, immortal person in Christ Jesus). What a blessing to be so distinctly separated from sin! What a blessing to know that motivation to sin is not generated in me! What a blessing to know that I am 100% loyal and faithful to Christ in my new man! What a freedom from guilt and what great motivation to fellowship with Christ, my Lord. The sinless Lord and my sinless being can walk together in perfect harmony because there is no sin to separate us!

But what about the sin of the flesh? Even though we may not be responsible for its presence we are certainly responsible for its control. That's right! We must learn to walk in the spirit. We must learn to appropriate Christ's presence in every expression of life if we are to control the expression of sin through the flesh! And we cannot always be in a spirit of appropriating Christ, so sooner or later the flesh will produce overt acts of sin. Carnality will sooner or later express itself through the flesh. What can be done about the expression of sin through the flesh? Aren't we responsible for that sin? Yes, we are, but we also are constantly being cleansed of the sin in the flesh. Without asking, as some teach, from I John 1:9 and just because Jesus Christ is faithful as a great high priest and just because his precious blood is ever present before the throne of God the sin of the flesh both the intrinsic presence and the overt expression of sin is being perpetually cleansed from the flesh by the ministry of Jesus Christ, the great high priest. Hebrews 7:25.

We, thus, always possess a clean vessel in our flesh with which to live with Christ, our Lord. There is no guilt of sin because the new man is dead to sin! There is no guilt of sin because flesh is cleansed from sin continuously. I John 1:7, Hebrews 7:25, I Peter 1:2, Romans 8:3, Romans 6:2, I John 2:2, Hebrews 10:17, Hebrews 8:12, Romans 6:7, Romans 6:11.

I once talked with a pentecostal minister about the security of the believer. I explained to him that contrary to his belief I believed that if we were really saved our salvation was eternal: to my surprise he told me he believed that he was also eternally saved! He then went on to explain that though he believed in the security of the believer he couldn't preach it from the pulpit for fear the congregation would take advantage of the teaching and begin to fall into sin!

No doubt some would feel this would also be the case by preaching the scriptural doctrine that we are "dead to sin." Romans 6:2. There really is no danger in preaching our complete liberty from sin, however, because "anyone who is *born of God does not* and *cannot* sin." I John 3:9. This, however, is a dangerous doctrine for a mere professor of Christianity for he will certainly take the liberty of sinning because of his "freedom." II Peter 2:22.

B. The Christian who is able to believe the scriptural teaching on the true essence of Christian being now discovers a new congruity of scriptures. He is no longer required to add or subtract from the scriptures to produce an agreement with the traditional concepts of Christian essence.

Illustration #1. In Romans 7:14-25 Paul is not recounting his experience as an unregenerate as some would suggest who cannot perceive the essence of the Christian experience, but is speaking as a mature Christian of his experience as a "new man" in a body of sinful flesh. Paul is not speaking as an immature Christian who has been unable to control the influence of the flesh. He is simply describing the distinct separation of his spirit and his flesh and the influence that the flesh and sin which indwells the flesh has upon his "new man."

Some have suggested that Paul has lost control or is under the control of the flesh, as though he is helpless to control the affect of sin in the flesh over his life. Such is not the case here! The context of chapters 6-7-8 make it clear that he is not in despair but is recognizing that he doesn't have a 100% freedom to act in the spirit! The flesh may exercise varying amounts of influence over the spirit but it never gains 100% influence over the spirit or the 8th chapter would make no sense. One is unsaved who walks "after the flesh" is "carnally minded" or is "in the flesh." One who is unsaved who is "under the control of sin" as some have suggested that Paul is saying is his condition in Romans 7:14-25.

Neither is Paul describing a dualism in his soul as others teach. For there to be a dualism there must of a sense be an equality of powers existing in his soul and such is not the case. He is simply describing the affect that sinful flesh exerts on his new man. He is aware of the battle between his spirit and his flesh, but he is also aware of the promise of deliverance from the flesh in Romans 8:11 and of the freedom from the bondage of fear through his new spiritual identity in Romans 8:14-18 as a son of God. He exults in the liberation of creation and even his own body from the affects of sin. Romans 8:19-23. And then, he ascends to the highest joy in confidence as he speaks of irrefutable justification and absolutely unfailing love of Christ. Romans 8:28-39. Romans 7:14-25 simply explains the battle between the spirit and the flesh much as does Galatians 5:16-17.

Romans 7:14-25 is Paul's description of the experience of a mature, spirit-led Christian as he observes the conflict of interest between his "new man" in Christ and the flesh in which he must live until he is set free by death or the rapture of the church.

The context of Romans chapter 5-8 fits together like this: With the center thought of the book of Romans being the "Gospel of God," Romans 1:1, Paul describes the amazing, almost overwhelming dynamics of the power of justification by faith in chapter 5. The thought of the grace of God is so overpowering in chapter 5 that it might cause one to usurp his privileges under grace and turn to a life of sin because of it! This is only a hypothetical conclusion, however, for Paul at chapter 6 begins to describe the true essence of Christian being. A true child of God is incapable of thinking that way and for several reasons.

First of all, because he has died to sin, Romans 6:2, it's not a part of him anymore! He has no ability to sin (i.e. in his new man) cf. I John 3:9. His new man has been created for only one function, cf. Ephesians 2:10, "for good works." He doesn't know how to sin anymore; although the flesh is capable of performing sin it left uncontrolled by the "new man." The new man is unable to plan or execute sin.

Secondly, he has died to self, Romans 6:3-10. The old man or old self was crucified and buried, Romans 6:6. This is the way one becomes a child of God in the first place: by total surrender of his life to Christ. Christ said, "except a corn of wheat falls into the ground and dies it abideth alone: but if it die, it bringeth forth much fruit." John 12:24.

Christ died to the affect of sin on his mortal body. That

is, he permitted his mortal body to be taken by sinful men and crucified on a cross in a dark sinful world. But when he arose from the grave he arose in a body that was incapable of being affected by sinful men or a sinful world. Likewise, our new "spiritual man" has arisen from the crucifixion of the old man and is incapable of being affected by sinful men or a sinful world. cf. verse 10.

Then, in verses 11-23 Paul tells us that all we need to do to prove that such a new man has arisen from the crucifixion of the old man is to experiment with our new life. As, by faith, cf. Romans 6:11, we believe we have a new man that is dead to sin living in the fleshly body, we are able to control the actions of the body. We are now able to actually become servants of God. See verse 22.

Paul continues to reinforce the thought of our separation from the old man by reminding us that we are separated from the law. Romans 7:1-6. Verse 4 says we are dead to the law in a way similar to the legality that separates a woman from her dead husband and allows here to be married to another. And, in like manner, we are married to Christ and separated from the law. Therefore, we are no longer obligated to the law in any way. In Romans 7:7-14 Paul teaches that the law is holy, just and good but that it can be used by an unsaved person, because of indwelling sin, to falsely justify his life with God. That same high standard of morality expressed by the law also reveals sin in the flesh of the Christian. However, in verses 15-25 Paul makes it very clear that the sin *is* in the flesh and not in the "new man."

Chapter 8 begins with the reminder that we are separated from judgement through Christ. We are also separated from sin and death through Christ. Also, we are separated from sin in the flesh by new life in Christ, 8:3-4.

In Romans 8:5-13, Paul warns that this blessed separation from sin, death, judgement and sin in the flesh is only for those who are spiritual: indeed, for those who walk after the spirit and not after the flesh.

He then describes the experience of new life in Christ as a sonship in God that is free from fear and bondage. Romans 8:14-17.

Then in verses 18-27 he reminds believers that this freedom from bondage won't be absolute and complete until we are separated from our mortal flesh and are indwelling resurrection flesh.

Then, finally, he begins at verse 28 through to the end of the chapter to exult in an expression of the victories of new life in Christ in predestination, justification, and the unfailing love of Christ for his own.

Romans, chapter 7, is not, as many have suggested, a parenthetical passage out of context in chapters 5-8, but a continuation of the revelation of the "new man" in Christ. he is a "new man" who is incapable of usurping the grace of God, who is learning, because of the new life within to subjugate the members of his body. He is a "new man" who is completely separated from the law as a motivation to live a holy life because he has the "Holy One Himself" living within. He is a "new man" who values the holiness of the law to reveal sin in the flesh but then is taught by the beloved apostle that he is separated from that sin by the new creation.

He is a "new man" who has discovered he is freed from sin, death, and sin in the flesh, whose direction for living is directed by the Holy Spirit and who is waiting for the ultimate deliverance from the flesh while experiencing the unfailing love of Christ in a body of sinful flesh.

Thus, Romans chapters 5 to 8 flows naturally through an explanation of the new life experience which results from the experience of justification by faith as explained in the first four chapters. The truth of scripture flows smoothly and naturally as one would expect from the mind of the apostle so we no longer need to wrestle with parenthetical, traditional explanations of Romans 7. Also, the true concept of Christian essence is liberating and faith-building for these dark days of increased faithlessness and apostasy. Praise the Lord!

Illustration #2. I John 3:9, I John 5:18.

I John 3:9 has been mentioned several times as a proof text for the sinless condition of the "new man." The translation of this verse provides a most astounding evidence of the affect of tradition upon truth. The Greek word, "poiei" which means "to make" or "to do" has also a very wide application in the Greek language. However, in my opinion the King James translators who ordinarily were quite literal, i.e. word for word equivalents, inserted an extra word in this verse which is unnecessary and also deterimental to the understanding of the verse. The word, "commit" was added without a Greek equivalent. The word, do or as King James translates, "doth" is a good equivalent for "poiei." "Commit" could be used by the criteria of wide application but not both words for a single Greek word. This unfortunate insertion of the word, "commit" has led to the interpretation of this verse as meaning those who are born of God do not practice sin as a general condition of their life. However, the verse literally says, "Everyone having been begotten of God *does not sin.* To interpret the first part of I John 3:9 otherwise is to violate the context of the verse because it continues by saying, "because his seed, (i.e. God's seed) remains in him and he cannot sin because he has been begotten of God." Did you get that? He *cannot sin!* He does not have the power to sin! This verse emphatically tells us that the born again (i.e. the new man) *does not sin* and *he cannot sin* because he is born of God. The flesh is not born of God so it sins because sin dwells in the flesh but the "new man" the "new creation," that which is born of God *cannot sin.*

I have twelve different translations of the New Testament in my library and only two of them translate I John 3:9 correctly.

I am convinced that the unfortunate Authorized Version translation of I John 3:9 plus the overall traditional concept of the two-nature interpretation of Christian essence has reproduced the error in most of the translations of the New Testament. I recommend that anyone unfamiliar with the Greek language secure an *"Interlinear Greek-English New Testament"* to verify the translation problem in this verse in both grammar and context. In my opinion, the Reverand Alfred Marshall D. Litt in his *"The Interlinear Greek-English New Testament"* has correctly translated this verse.

In addition to I John 3:9, I John 5:18 repeats the same truth. "We know that everyone having been begotten of God sins not, but the one begotten . . . God keeps him, and the evil one does not touch him."[1]

A Christian, then, on the one hand, must confess that he has sin and that he has sinned, I John 1:8,9, as he considers the awareness of his "new man" bound in a body of sinful flesh. And, yet, he can also from the same epistle of John declare that he does not sin, and he cannot sin because of the new birth as he considers only that spiritual immortal part of his being. It all depends on whether he is considering the "new man" only, or the "new man" imprisoned in "flesh."

Please refer to my diagrams, earlier in this chapter, pages 37 & 38 that illustrate the centers of awareness as a Christian walks in the spirit or fulfills the lust of the flesh.

Another interesting evidence of the existence of the "new man" and the death of the "old man" is the description of the battle between the spirit and the flesh in Galatians 5:16. A Christian may "walk" in the spirit but he cannot "walk" in the flesh because there is no "old man" present in

---

[1]The Reverend Alfred Marshall D. Litt, *The Interlinear Greek-English New Testament,* p. 946

which he may walk. He can fulfill the lust of the flesh only if he is not walking in spirit. If his center of awareness is spiritual he will not allow the flesh to express the sin that indwells it. If, through the many distractions of life, he allows his brain to center on fleshly things he will eventually perform sinful acts from the flesh. They key to victorious Christ-honoring Christian life, then, is not fighting sin, or controlling the old man, but walking in the fellowship and guidance of the indwelling Christ. If a Christian attempts to control sin in the flesh by the will of the flesh he will fall into an entanglement with sin, much as a fly that struggles to free itself from a spider web becomes more entagled as it struggles to free itself. Therefore, fellowship with Christ, the highest and most blessed experience of Christian living not only produces an effective, productive life but eliminates the possibility of expressing sin from the flesh.

Chapter 2

The Expression of God's Love

*O*ne of the most universally taught doctrines in the church today is the concept that God loves the unsaved. The big surprise concerning this teaching is that it has a traditional rather than a scriptural origin. This traditional doctrine finds its expression in a typical evangelical emphasis in such expressions as, "God loves you and has a wonderful plan for your life." It is often seen on bumper stickers declaring, "Smile, God loves you." Perhaps some hasty conclusions drawn from John 3:16 and an intense concern for an acceptable message that wouldn't be offensive to the lost have brought about this erroneous expression of God's love. It's difficult to bluntly preach "he that believeth not is condemned already" John 3:18 K.J. and "he that believeth not the Son shall not see life; but the wrath of God abideth on him" John 3:36 K.J. c.f. also, Romans 1:18, 2:5, 2:8-9, Romans 9:11-13, 22. Yet, truthfully, this should be the message to the lost so they might fear and repent rather than be lulled into a complacency by an indulging God who purportedly loves them.

For the Christian, this is a true Biblical doctrine, but

for the unsaved who will never make that life-saving decision to receive Jesus Christ as Lord and Savior it finds no scriptural support! It is not true now for an unbeliever, nor will it ever be true for one who rejects Jesus Christ.

For a doctrine to be Biblical and not traditional it must find substantial support in the Word. This doctrine has no scriptural support that I can find.

In John 8:44 Jesus calls the unbelieving Jews the children of the devil. He also separates believers from unbelievers in John 17:16 as He says of the "men" which had been given to him out of the world (John 17:6), "They are not of the world even as I am not of the world." All unbelievers fall into the category of the world and the devil's children for he is the god of this world.

To say that God loves the sinner or God loves the sinner and hates his sin is an unscriptural rationalization when speaking of those who will never receive eternal life through Jesus Christ.

The Bible is unwavering in its declaration that "He that believeth on the Son hath everlasting life: and he that believeth not the Son shall not see life: *But the wrath of God abideth on him." c.f. John 3:36.*

There is no way that we can rationalize the clear declaration of God's wrath remaining on the disobedient as a future experience rather than a present experience. The exercise of God's wrath on unbelievers is a future event but His feeling toward them is a present experience. c.f. Romans 2:5.

Beyond the fact that such teaching finds no scriptural base, it compromises the morality of God in that He condones sin without justification. Therefore, the doctrine impugns the character and holiness of God who exacts punishment for sin, c.f. Ezekiel 18:4, 20; Matthew 25:41, 46; John 5:29; Romans 2:5-11; IIThessalonians 1:7-9; Hebrews 10:28-31; IIPeter 2:9; Jude 14:15; Revelation

20:11-15; Revelation 21:8.

If an unbelieving Christ-rejecting person is told that God loves him just as he is, he will assume that it is probably unnecessary to become a Christian since if God loves him, the threat of punishment for rejecting Christ is just a ploy by God to get him to surrender his life. Surely, God wouldn't condemn to eternal hell anyone He loves. He, thus, has no real motivation to become a Christian.

What is Love?

A. The Dictionary definition.

In seeking to define the concept of love, Webster's Dictionary[1] says, "1 a: affection based on admiration or benevolence b. an assurance of love. 2a: a warm attachment, enthusiasm, or devotion b: the object of such attachment or devotion 3A: unselfish concern that freely accepts another in loyalty and seeks his good: (1) the fatherly concern of God for man (2) brotherly concern for others b: Man's adoration of God 4a: the attraction based on sexual desire: the affection and tenderness felt by lovers b: a god or per-sonification of love c: an amorous episode: Love Affair d: sexual embrace: Copulation 5a: beloved per-son: Darling 6a: a score of zero in tennis 7: cap, Chris-tian Science: GOD." In the verb form Webster's defines love as "1: to hold dear: Cherish 2a: to feel a lover's passion, devotion or gentleness for b: Caress 3: to like or desire actively: take pleasure in 4: to thrive in: to feel affection or experience desire."

Although we may not endorse all the theological aspects of Webster's definition the general definition of love as a benevolent affection toward another is also a good

---

[1]Webster's Seventh New Collegiate Dictionary.

general Biblical definition for love.

B. A Biblical definition.

The word, love, according to Strong's Concordance occurs 129 times in the Old Testament and is translated from 8 Hebrew words. The word, love, occurs 173 times in the New Testament and is translated from 12 Greek words.

The word, loved, occurs 56 times in the Old Testament and is translated by 3 Hebrew words. In the New Testament "loved" occurs 41 times and is translated by 3 Greek words.

The greatest number of occurrences of the word, love, in the Old Testament is translated from Strong's Concordance #157, #160 the Hebrew word "aw-hab" or "aw-habe" which means "to have affection for."

Other occurrences are defined as: to love, to cling, to join, love, amative words, amorousness, to fondle, to compassionate, a female associate.

In the New Testament the greatest number of occurrences of the word, love, is the Greek word, "agape" and its verb form. Strong's #25 & 26. Its' meaning is affection or benevolence.

Other New Testament uses are defined as: to choose or prefer or wish, to be a friend, to have affection, a fraternal affection, fond of brethren, avarice or love of money, fond of man, fond of one's children.

In summarizing the definition of the word, love, from both the secular and the Biblical point of view we must agree that it is defined, generally, as *a personal affection of benevolence toward another person* with varying shades of meaning depending on the kind of personal involvement.

In a view of both the secular and biblical definitions, love is a personal thing and the question of God's personal involvement with and affection for the unsaved is the question that is raised in such slogans as "Smile, God loves you." Does He love all men, saved and unsaved alike with an affection of personal benevolence? If so, where does the scripture describe this affection?

The expression, "God loves you," is used so commonly in preaching and teaching today that it is difficult to believe that the Bible makes no statement concerning God loving the unsaved! And, in fact, statements concerning the anger and wrath of God for the unsaved are found throughout scripture.

It is for this reason that I want to list *every* scripture in the Bible that speaks of God's love to show that the doctrine is traditional and not scriptural.

BIBLICAL RESEARCH ON THE WORDS LOVE, LOVED using Strong's Exhaustive Concordance, pages 637, 638.

Strong's#	Scripture	Object of Love
1. 2836	Deut.7:7-9	God loves the Israel that loves Him
2. 157	Deut.7:12-13	God loves obedient Israel
3. 157	Prov.8:17	God loves those who love Him
4. 2836	Isa.38:17	God loved Hezekiah's soul
5. 157	Isa.61:8	God loves judgement
6. 160	Isa. 63.9	God loves redeemed Israel
7. 160	Jere.31:3	God loves the remnant of Israel cf.vs.7
8. 160	Hosea 3:1	God loves a seeking, fearing, forgiven Israel cf.vs.5
9. 157	Hosea 14:4	God loves a forgiven Israel cf.vs.2
10. 160	Zeph.3:17	God will rest in His love over redeemed Israel

In the O.T. there are 14 scriptures that reveal that which God loved.

Strong's#	Scripture	Object of Love
1. 160	Deut.7:8	God loved the Israel that love Him cf.vs.9
2. 157	Deut.23:5	God loved Israel
3. 2245	Deut.33:3	God loved the people, His saints
4. 157	IISam.12:24	God loved Solomon
5. 160	IKings10:9	God loved Israel forever
6. 160	IIChron.2:11	God loved His people
7. 160	IIChron.9:8	God loved Israel
8. 157	Ps.47:4	God loved Jacob
9. 157	Ps.78:68	God loved the tribe of Juda, the mount Zion
10. 157	Isa.43:4	God loved the redeemed of Israel
11. 157	Isa.48:14	God loved Jacob and Israel
12. 157	Jere.31:3	God loved all the families of Israel
13. 157	Hos.11:1	God loved Israel
14. 157	Mal.1:2	God loved Israel

In all 24 O.T. passages which reveal that which God loves or loved there is not one single reference to His either loving or having loved the unsaved or the nations of the world. 22 of the 24 references relate His love for redeemed Israel or her kings. 1 reference declares He loves justice and 1 reference declares His love for those who love Him.

In the N.T. there are 26 scriptures revealing that which God loves.

Strong's#	Scripture	Object of Love
1. 25	John 10:17	The Father loves the son
2. 25	John 14:21	Christ will love those who love Him
3. 25	John 14:23	The Father will love those who love Christ
4. 25	John 15:9	Christ loves us as the Father loved Him
5. 26	John 15:10	Christ will love us if we keep His commandments
6. 26	John 15:10	Christ who has kept the Father's commandments abides in His love

7.	26	Rom.5:8*D	God displayed (commends or recommends His love; lexicon = to place in a striking point of view Grk. "soon-is-tah's") His love in Christ's death on the cross for sinners.
8.	26	Rom.8:35	Christ loves those who love God cf. vs. 28
9.	26	Rom.8:39	God loves those in Christ Jesus our Lord
10.	26	IICor.13:14	God loves Christian brethren
11.	26	Eph.2:4*P	God exercises His love on the predestined saved
12.	26	Eph. 3:19	Christ loves all saints
13.	26	IIThes.3:5	God loves the brethren
14.	26	ITim.1:14-15*P	The faith and love of God in super-abounding grace predestined through the cross of Christ saved Paul
15.	26	IITim.1:13	Christ Jesus loves Timothy
16.	5363	Tit.3:4-5*P	God's love appeared through Jesus Christ
17.	26	IJn.2:15	The Father's love is *not* in those who love the world
18.	26	IJn. 3:1	God's kind of love produces children of God
19.	26	IJn.3:16	We first experienced God's love through faith in Christ's sacrifice for us
20.	26	IJn.3:17	God's love does *not* remain in anyone who will not help a brother in need
21.	26	IJn.4:9-10*P	God revealed His love through the sacrifice of His Son
22.	25	IJn.4:12	God's love matures in Christians if they love one another
23.	26	IJn.4:16	God's love as well as God's person indwells the one who confesses that Jesus is the Son of God
24.	26	IIJn.3	The Father and the Son love the children of truth
25.	26	Jude 21	God loves whose who wait on the mercy of the Lord Jesus Christ
26.	5368	Rev.3:19	The Lord loves those that He rebukes and chastens (the children of God. cf.Heb.12:5-6)

In survey of the New Testament scriptures which reveal the object of God's love we must conclude that the persons of the Holy Trinity are objects of each other's love. Secondly, there are numerous scriptures that reveal God's love for the faithful children of God. Thirdly, a number of verses describe an impersonal display (cf. D on previously listed verses) of God's love through the death of Christ on the cross. Fourthly, the actual exercise of God's love is first experienced in the process of spiritual rebirth through faith in Christ's death on the cross. Finally, (cf. P on the previously listed verses) God's love may be expressed by Him in predestination. In other words, God is able to love that which He knows shall be, before it exists. An illustration of predestined love is found in Ephesians 5:25, "Husbands, love your wives, as *Christ loved the church,* and gave Himself for it." This verse tells us that Christ *loved* the church as a past tense and yet even at this time the church is still incomplete and will be incomplete until the rapture occurs. However, not one single reference suggests any personal love of God for the unsaved. The only experience the unsaved have of God's love is the display of the love in the cross of Christ. Just as a drowning man may see a rope close by held by a man on shore and refuse to accept help, so those who refuse by faith to take hold of the substitutionary death of Christ on the cross will never feel the tugs from the life preserving power of God.

To complete the study on the expression of God's love it will be necessary to examine the New Testament scriptures that reveal things that God has loved.

In the N.T. there are 29 scriptures that reveal things that God has loved.

Strong's#	Scripture	Object Loved
1. 25	Mark 10:21	Jesus loved one (cf.footnote #1) who kneeled before Him.

2.	25	Jn.3:16	God loved the world (cf.footnote #2)
3.	25	Jn.11:5	Jesus loved Martha and Mary
4.	25	Jn.13:1	Jesus loved His own
5.	25	Jn.13:23	Jesus loved one of His disciples
6.	25	Jn.13:34	Jesus loved His disciples
7.	25	Jn.14:21	Those that love Christ shall be loved by the Father
8.	25	Jn.15:9	The Father loved Christ and Christ loved the disciples
9.	25	Jn.15:12	Christ loved His disciples
10.	25	Jn.17:23	God loved the disciples as He loved Christ
11.	25	Jn. 17:26	God loved Christ
12.	25	Jn.19:26	Jesus loved His disciples, John
13.	1568	Jn. 20:2	Jesus loved His disciple, John
14.	25	Jn.21:7	Jesus loved His disciple, John
15.	25	Jn.21:20	Jesus loved His disciple, John cf.21:24
16.	25	Rom. 8:37	Jesus Christ loved them that loved God
17.	25	Rom.9:13	God loved Jacob
18.	25	Gal.2:20	Christ loved Paul
19.	25	Eph.2:4-5*P	God loved the spiritually reborn
20.	26	Eph.5:2	Christ loved God's children
21.	25	Eph.5:25*P	Christ loved the church
22.	25	IIThes.2:16	Christ and the Father loved the saints
23.	25	Heb.1:9	Christ loved righteousness
24.	25	IJn.4:10*P	God's love manifested in Christ's death (v.9) to unbelievers became the experience of God's love to believers. God loved us (believers) through the manifestation of His love to the world.
25.	25	IJn.4:11*P	God loved the saints
26.	25	IJn.4:19*P	God loved the saints
27.	25	Rev.1:5*P	Christ loved those He washed in His own blood
28.	25	Rev.3:9	Christ loved the saints at the church at Philadelphia
29.	25	Jn.17:24	God loved the son before the foundation of the world

In a survey of the New Testament scriptures that

reveal the things that God has loved we discover that in 23 of the 29 occurences of the word, "loved," the object of His love is His disciples. He also loved the world, Christ, Jacob, the Church and righteousness. In no case is it ever said that God loves the unbeliever or the sinner or the unsaved.

Note #1

One may argue that the "rich young ruler" was unsaved (Mark 10:21) "so here is the exception to the rule." There is no scripture to indicate that he was unsaved. In fact, there is very strong evidence for his faith in that:
  (a) He was in quest of eternal life
  (b) He kneeled to Jesus Christ
  (c) He called him *good* master cf.vs.18
  (d) He was obedient to the law
  (e) Though he was grieved by the request to sell all he had and give to the poor and follow Christ there is no scripture to indicate that he did not follow these directions. How many believers of our day could measure up to this standard of faith?

Note #2 An Interpretation of John 3:16

In John 3:16 the scripture says that "God so loved the *world* that He gave His only begotten Son." "If God loved the world doesn't that include the unsaved?" The answer is, yes, if we think of this complex world system in which we are now living for the unsaved are a part of this present world, material universe, aggregate of mankind, the public, present order of things, human race, etc. But let us remind ourselves that the scriptures also teach that Satan is the god of this world, Luke 4:5-6, IICor.4:4, John 14:30 and demons inhabit this world, Mark 5:1-16, Eph.6:12, therefore, if God loves this present world He must also love Satan and the demons, for they are a part of this world.

Why, then, are we warned in I John 2:15 not to love the world if God loves the world? The only logical and scriptural answer is that God is not in love with this present evil world and the unsaved people who are part of it.

However, according to John 3:16 God has loved the world at sometime before Christ spoke these words to Nicodemus or the verse is not true.

The question that logically follows is, "Was there ever a time or a world that God could love?" and, the answer is, yes, if we go back to the very beginning of creation.

In Genesis 1:10, 12, 18, 21 and 25, God remarks in the completion of various stages of creation that "it was good." Finally, in Genesis 1:31 His commentary on the whole of creation was that "It was very good."

God had a plan for creation and for man (Gen.1:26-27, Ps.8) which was destroyed by Satan and sin and the curse upon man and creation. cf.Gen.3:14-19.

God is able to love good things and by His own admission everything that he created was good. It was exactly what he had planned.

However, God so loved "that originally created world" that He gave in predestination His only begotten Son (cf. the promise, Gen.3:15) that whosoever believeth in Him should not perish but have everlasting life. This is the only interpretation possible in view of the context of the objects of God's love and the holiness and character of God.

The word, lovest, in connection with the things God loves occurs only once in the Old Testament.

Strong's#	Scripture	Object of God's Love
1. 157	Ps.45:7	Christ loves righteousness cf.Heb.1:8,9

The word, lovest, in connection with the things God loves, occurs only once in the New Testament.

Strong's#	Scripture	Object of God's Love
1. 5368	John 11:3	Christ is loving Lazarous

The word, loves, in connection with the things God loves, occurs 8 times in the Old Testament.

Strong's#	Scripture	Object of God's Love
1. 157	Deut.10:18	God loves the stranger
2. 157	Ps.11:7	God loves the righteous
3. 157	Ps.33:5	God loves the righteous
4. 157	Ps.37:28	God loves judgment
5. 157	Ps.87:2	God loves the gates of Zion
6. 157	Ps.146:8	God loves the righteous
7. 157	Prov.3:12	God loves those He corrects
8. 157	Prov.15:9	God loves those who follow after righteousness

Note on #1 stranger = there is no indication from scripture that a stranger is an unsaved person for strangers or proselytes were received into the camp of Israel and included in the blessings of Israel. cf. Ex.12:19,48; Lev. 19:34.

The word, loves, in connection with the things God loves, occurs 5 times in the New Testament.

Strong's#	Scripture	Object of God's Love
1. 25	Jn.3:35	God loves the Son
2. 5368	Jn.5:20	God loves the Son
3. 5368	Jn.16:27	God loves you (the disciples)
4. 25	IICor.9:7	God loves a cheerful giver
5. 25	Heb.12:6	God loves those He chastens

III. Summary

In summarizing the Biblical research on the expression of God's love we have discovered:

1. That of the 479 uses of the word, love, in the bible,

93 references relate to God's love. About 1 in 5 references to love in the Bible relate to God's love. Therefore, the expression of God's love is not an obscure doctrine of scripture.

2. In all of the 93 references to God's love not one single reference specifically names the unsaved as the object of God's love.

3. In 73 of the 93 references to God's love the saved are specifically named as the object of God's love.

4. There are certain conditions which so limit the expression of God's love that no unsaved person could qualify as the object of God's love. These conditions for the expression of God's love are:

a. In the Old Testament:

(1) God loves the Israel that *loves* Him. cf. Deut. 7:7-9 vs.9 "Which keepeth covenant and mercy with them that love Him and His commandments." cf. also Prov.8:17.

(2) God loves Israel that *keeps His commandments.* cf. Deut.7:9; Prov.15.9 Since only those who love and *obey* God are loved by Him, the unsaved are excluded from God's love.

(3) God loves *those He corrects.* Prov.3:12 There is no indication from scripture that God *corrects* the Devil's children.

b. The condition for the expression of God's love in the New Testament are:

(1) John 14:21 – God will love all those who *love* Christ.

(2) John 14:21 – God will love all those who *obey* Christ. cf. also John 14:23,24; John 15:9,10; Rom.8:28 & 35 & 39

(3) IICor.9:7 – God loves a *cheerful giver.*

(4) Heb.12:6 – God loves *those he chastens.*

(5) IJn.2:15 – God *will not love* those who love the world.

(6) IJn.3:17 – God *will not love* those who do not show love to their brethren.

In view of these six conditions for the expression of God's love it is apparent that God loves the saved and cannot, because of these conditions, love the unsaved.

The traditional doctrine that declares that God loves the sinner or the unsaved, especially as it relates to those not predestined to eternal life, has several deterimental affects.

(1) It undermines the concept of the holiness and majesty of the Godhead to the unsaved and brings God down from the heavens to compromise Himself in a fellowship of love with sinners. cf. Rom.1:21-23

(2) It undermines the motivation for salvation from the consequences of sin to the unsaved in that they really have nothing to fear from a God who loves them. Prov.1:7

(3) It establishes an irrational expression of God's love in that He expresses love without discernment.

(4) It demoralizes the love of the saved for God and limits the reciprocation of their love for God in that God's love for them is common to both saved and unsaved alike.

(5) And last of all, and perhaps the most important of all, is that to say that God loves all men both saved and unsaved alike, is a direct contradiction of scripture.

The scriptures indicate that God has feelings for the unsaved but that love is not one of them.

In the Old Testament as in the new Testament the words *anger* and *wrath* are similar in meaning. They may be defined as rapid breathing, violent passions, exasperation and outburst. The word, anger, is used about 300 times in the Old Testament and about 12 times in the New Testament. the word, wrath, is used about 190 times in the Old Testament and 75 times in the New. These words are often used to describe God's feelings toward the unsaved and, in the Old Testament, only, are often used to describe His feelings toward Israel and even Moses. However, in the New Testament the words are never used to describe God's feelings toward the saved or the Church. In fact, many uses of the word, wrath, in conjunction with the saved are expressions in which we are said to have been saved from God's wrath through Christ. cf.Rom.5:9; IThess.1:10; IThess.5:9.

On the other hand, the unsaved are said to have God's wrath upon them. cf. John 3:36; Rom.1:18; Rom.2:5; Rom.2:8; Rom.4:15; Rom.9:22; Eph.5:6; Eph.2:3; Col. 3:6; IThess.2:16; Heb.3:11; Rev.6:17; Rev.11:18; Rev. 14:10; Rev.14:19; Rev.15:1; Rev. 15:7; Rev.16:1; Rev. 18:3; Rev.19:15.

The scriptures indicate that God is presently experiencing feelings of wrath toward the unsaved cf.John 3:36; Rom.2:5; Rom.9:22; Eph.5:6; Col.3:6 and that these pent up feelings of God's wrath will ultimately be unleashed in the "day of judgement." cf.Rom.2:5; IThess.1:10; Rev. 6:17.

In view of the many scriptures that teach that God has feelings of wrath for the unsaved rather than feelings of love and that no scripture teaches that God loves the unsaved it is surprising that evangelists persist in preaching to many who through disobedience and rejection of Christ will never know God's love or that "God loves them and has a wonderful plan for their life."

Some verses I have marked with an asterik to denote the probability that in the foreknowledge of God He may be able to love the believer in advance of his belief but as experiencing him as His son in foreknowledge.

Romans 8:29 describes those who are foreknown to also be formed in the image of Christ, called justified and glorified.

In Romans 9, verses 12 and 13 also link foreknowledge with the predetermined feelings of God. If God is able to love in advance of the life experience He, then, is also able to hate in advance of the life experience depending on foreknowledge for His feeling.

In no case, however, does the Scripture describe God as loving one who uniformly rejects Christ or is classified as an unbeliever.

Now that you have competed the reading of this chapter, and the evidence from scripture itself concerning the expression of God's love you are probably surprised and overwhelmed by the abundance of evidence that refutes the traditional teaching "that God loves the sinner but hates his sin." This teaching has been taught so much that you will have a real difficulty believing the truth. If you will carefully study each scripture reference presented in this chapter you will be able, by the scripture itself to see that this is an error of tradition and not the truth of the scripture.

As a Christian, you will be more devoted to God who really loves you with a discerning love, and more effective as an evangelist in telling the lost they have much to fear from God's wrath.

Chapter 3

The Unconditional Cleansing of Sin

*I*t has been systematically taught that God provides cleansing of all sin to an unbeliever who places his faith in the substitutionary death of Christ on the cross and that faith in his blood for the propitiation of sin is complete and absolute. However, because the believer sins after his initial and complete cleansing, to restore him back into fellowship with God, it is necessary to confess his sins on a regular basis to maintain fellowship with God. The basis for this doctrine of fellowship maintainance is found in only one verse of New Testament scriptures: Namely, I John 1:9.

There are, upon careful examination of this text, several reasons to suspect much error in this interpretation which not only is a discredit to the Word of God, but rob the believer of a sense of security in the propitiatory blood of Jesus Christ and diminish the faith of Christian experience.

The interpretation of the passage, as well as all sound biblical interpretation, depends on an examination of the scripture in its context, and as well, a careful examination of its grammar.

The context of I John 1:9 should, first of all, be considered in the context of the book of 1st John. The principle passage on the purpose of writing the book is 5:13. John declares, "I wrote these things to you in order that you might know that you have eternal life, to the ones believing in the name of the Son of God." In other words, "I want you to experience the assurance of your salvation in Jesus Christ." We would from this clear declaration of his purpose in writing the book then expect to find ample information to assure us that we really do possess eternal life. We would also expect that the information contained in the book would be directed toward proving that we, in fact, possess eternal life and can really *know* it.

It is interesting to note that generally commentaries on I John suggest for a purpose of writing by John, the apostle, such things as an emphasis on Christian fellowship, a family letter, want of brotherly love, to refute the beginnings of a Docetic, heretical tendancy in the churches, and to refute the beginnings of a Gnostic tendancy in the churches.

I have been amazed that such purposes of writing have been espoused in view of the clear statement by John in 5:13, "I wrote these things that you may know that you have eternal life." It is no doubt true that the content of I John provides answers to the heresy of the day but the emphasis is more on *"knowing"* that one possesses eternal life than on any specific refutation of doctrinal error. The characteristics of one who is truly a child of God are repeatedly compared to the characteristics of one who is not a child of God but professes to be.

In I John 2:4 the description of one who professes to know Christ and doesn't keep the commandments is compared to the description of one who really knows Christ and keeps his word. In 2:9 & 10 love for the brethren is true evidence of salvation while hate for the brethren is sure evidence of being unsaved. This theme is amplified in 3:11-15 where hating a brother is equated to murder and "that no murderer has eternal life abiding in him."

If one misses the central purpose for the writing of this epistle he will, no doubt, have a difficult time understanding the meaning of I John 1:9. However, in the context of discerning a true believer from a mere professor and examining the characteristics of the life of a true believer with one who claims to be a Christian but is not, we see a series of comparisons between a true believer and a mere professor in Chapter one, verses 6-10. Verse 9 is not some kind of an admonition to sanctification as has been generally taught, but describes the characteristcs of a true believer. That is, the true believer admits that he has sins. If the word "since" were substituted for the word "if" in I John 1:9 the whole meaning of the verse opens to its true contextual meaning. "*Since* we confess our sins, he is faithful and just to forgive us our sins and to cleanse us from all unrighteousness." This forgiveness and cleansing from unrighteousness belongs only to the true believer. The professor of Christianity has no right to the legacy of the children of God. Not only do we have a complete and perfect forgiveness of our sins, but we have a continuous cleansing from all unrighteousness in our Christian lives. Although Christians "admit" or "confess" their sins while the unsaved say "we have no sin" or "we have not sinned" or we live just as good a life as you Christians do, this is by no means a complete evidence of salvation but is part of the complex of "circumstantial evidence" which differentiates between a "true believer" and a "professor."

It is no surprise, then, to find that the Holy Spirit, in moving John to confirm the believer's salvation would inspire the repetition of the word, "know" in the text of his letter. The word, "know" occurs forty times in this short epistle. The other usages of the word, "knoweth" and "known" add eleven more uses which tally fifty-one uses of the word, "know" in I John. Compared to other New Testament epistles, this is a much higher proportion per chapter than any other New Testament epistle. The word, "know," averages eight times per chapter in I John and has more occurrences here than any other New Testament epistle except the Gospel of John which as seventy occurrences for twenty-one chapters or an average of 3.3 times per chapter. Let there be no doubt that the theme of First John is assurance of salvation. All other references to the purpose of writing support the central theme of assurance of salvation.

Upon analyzing the epistle for such assurance of salvation we discover seventy-five pieces of evidence to convince a believer he is truly saved and thirty pieces of evidence to convince a "professor of christianity" that he is really not saved. Perhaps the number of pieces of evidence for and against salvation will vary depending on whether one deletes repetitions and whether or not the evidence is considered explicit or not, yet it becomes quite clear that this process of collecting and expressing information for the assurance of salvation is unique to the epistle of 1st John and supports the central theme and purpose of writing. It is with this context in mind that we are able to see a different interpretation of I John 1:9 from the traditional fellowship and sanctification theme to the truly victorious theme of unconditional cleansing as an adjunct to the assurance of salvation. The probability clauses beginning in verse 6 and extending through verse 10 are now seen to be purposefully used to separate those who profess salvation from those who possess salvation.

In the context of New Testament Scripture, the concept of the necessity of the confession of one's sins to God for forgiveness, as a believer, cannot be found. Therefore, this single verse is used as a proof text for a doctrine that is in fact contradictory to the balance of New Testament Scripture.

Elsewhere in the New Testament we have solid evidence that the question of the forgiveness of the believer's sin has been unconditionally cared for by the "once for all" sacrifice of shed blood and the priesthood of Christ who efficasiously applies the blood to the believers life as a faithful high priest. Hebrews 7:25 declares we are "saved entirely because he is always living to intercede on our behalf." There is no suggestion that we play any part in Christ's priestly ministry of cleansing.

Some commentators have suggested that the washing of the disciples feet in John 13 is an illustration of a positional and practical cleansing of a believer's sins. That is, that the believer is cleansed from all sin "once for all" but needs to bring his daily sins to the Father in confession to maintain an unbroken fellowship. But, however, we see nothing in this passage to suggest that the believer initiates any of the cleansing process! It is the *Savior* who girds himself with the towel and washes the disciples feet. *They make no request for cleansing,* and when Peter refuses the cleansing he is told he must accept the cleansing if he is to have a part with Jesus.

Additionally, many New Testament Scriptures teach unconditional cleansing and there is no suggestion that a different kind of "family cleansing" through confession is a part of the New Testament experience. cf. Romans 5:9, Ephesians 1:7, Colossians 1:14, Hebrews 9:14, Hebrews 13:12, 20-21, I John 1:7, Revelation 1:5, Revelation 5:9, Romans 6:2, Romans 6:11, I Peter 2:24.

Indeed, the concept of an absolute cleansing from sin apart from personal involvement is the standard of New Testament doctrine.

Sometimes the cleansing of Christ's blood is seen as an all-inclusive application of cleansing of sins committed before becoming a Christian, as well as those committed as a Christian. At other times, the scriptures refer to a cleansing of sin from the Christian's life. Acts 20:28 refers to the blood as the price of acquisition for the church. Romans

3:25 declares faith in the blood as totally propitious and effective for the purging of sins committed under the Old Testament which had only been atoned for by animal sacrifice. Romans 5:9 declares our justification is complete through his blood. I Corinthians 11:25 tells us the communion cup symbolizes the seal of his blood on the new covenant of promises of God.

However, Ephesians 1:7 and Colossians 1:14 seem to view the efficacy of the blood in two apsects. Ephesians 1:7 teaches the comprehensive affect of the blood in redemption and then adds forgiveness of trespasses or "falling aside" which is descriptive of a Christians relationship to sin rather than an unregenerate. There is no mention here of a believer's responsibility to confess in order to effect this cleansing!

The corelative passage in Colossians 1:14 also follows this theme of life cleansing for a Christian by reminding us that in Christ we have both redemption and the forgiveness of our sins. The forgiveness of *our* sins indicates that as Paul is writing to believers he is addressing the subject of believers sins. Also, the forgiveness of our *sins* indicates that he is addressing the subject of believers *sins*: not sin generically speaking.

Hebrews 9:14 teaches that the blood of Jesus Christ has the power to purge the believer's conscience from "dead works to serve the living God." How does this work? The answer is by believing that we are continuously cleansed from sin as Christians by the power of the blood and the faithfulness of our great high priest. (cf. Hebrews 7:25). Our minds are set free from the guilt of dead works to serve God. The obsession with confession syndrome binds the Christian life with introspection and guilt with which God never intended that we should be involved. Jesus paid it all: past sin, present sin, future sin and we need to trust his blood for complete cleansing and stop questioning the efficacy of the blood and the faithfulness of Jesus Christ, our high priest. Hebrews 10:29 warns against devaluing the power of the blood of Christ and thus insulting the Holy Spirit.

I Peter 1:2 also seems to be referring to blood sprinkling for cleansing of sin in the Christian life and I John 1:7, without a doubt, teaches total cleansing from sin, past, present and future.

The New Testament teaches an unconditional cleansing in which we are "dead to sin." That is, we have no more relationship with sin, and the knowledge of this absolute cleansing promotes a clean conscience which enables us to serve our God. cf. Hebrews 10:17-25, Hebrews 9:14.

The sin that resides in the flesh of the Christian life is not our concern but God's. If it were possible for us in any way by the exercise of our faith to enter into the ministry of the "Great High Priest," our Savior, we diminish His ministry of cleansing in our lives and thus cleanse ourselves of the sins of our flesh. In essence, we discredit not only the blood of Christ, thus making it affective only for original cleansing from sin at the time of salvation but we also discredit the priesthood of Christ in that we enter into the process of mediation for the cleansing of sin. Additionally, we reject the promise of the Father who promises to forget our sin, Hebrews 10:17, and through our prayer remind Him of the sin He has forgotten thus denying that He has really forgiven it. Likewise, we labor for Christ under a false guilt complex and are unable to perform in the fullness of faith when we use confession to give us psychological help from the guilt of sin that we are dead to and which has been forgiven and which God has forgotten.

If we should conceed that there is such a thing as "family sin" separate from original sin several questions need to be answered concerning this sin. The first question that needs to be asked concerning the confession of sins for the restoration of fellowship with God is what kind of sin must be confessed? If the answer is all sin then the next question is who makes the determination as to what sin *is* for that individual believer at that particular point in his life. We know the great commandment taught by our Savior is that "thou shalt love the Lord your God with all thy heart and soul and mind and the second is like unto it that thou shall love they neighbor as thyself." No one is capable of fulfilling the great commandment. Since we are constantly living in dereliction of our duty to love with *all* heart, *all* mind, and *all* soul we must constantly be in a state of confession. Then, since we cannot spend every waking moment in confession what happens to our fellowship if based on the confession of every sin?

If we write-off the great commandment and decide that we will only need to confess the sins that are apparent to us we must ask the question, "What about sins that are really inexcusable for a Christian but that haven't been brought to his attention?" Do these sins break fellowship? Then suppose that we were able to decide on a list of sins that a Christian should recognize as sin. What happens if we forget to confess one of them? Does this break fellowship? Another question that must be asked is, "If we in one of many ways fail to ask forgiveness of our sins are we living with unforgiven sin?" since I John 1:9 says "*if* we confess our sins He is faithful and just to forgive our sins and to cleanse us from all unrighteousness."

Another question then comes to mind. If we fail in the contract of confession and now have unforgiven sin in our lives how dangerous is this? Is this unforgiven sin powerful enough to cause us to lose our salvation? Can the unrighteous inherit eternal life? Without cleansing which results from confession we surely are unrighteous according to this interpretation of I John 1:9.

Still other questions arise from this interpretation of I John 1:9 concerning broken fellowship. What is meant by broken fellowship? Is it a loss of sonship? This could hardly be the meaning in the light of so much scripture which teaches the security of the believer.

Then, if we do not lose sonship in broken fellowship, what do we lose? Is there any scripture to describe any infringement of fellowship through a lack of confession?

A topical study of the word, "fellowship" reveals the word is only used 14 times in the New Testament. Not one of these references deals with the subject of a break in fellowship because of sin. No New Testament passage deals with a repair of fellowship through confession of sin. Christian fellowship with God is unrevokable and unchanging according to scriptures. I Corinthians 1:9 teaches an unfailing fellowship with God because of God's faithfulness, not ours. "God is faithful through whom we were called to the fellowship of His son Jesus Christ our Lord." There are no conditions to this fellowship! In I John 1:3 John triumphantly declares "Indeed our fellowship is with the Father and with his Son Jesus Christ." There are no conditions to fellowship. It is improper to subject the new covenant in Jesus Christ to the conditions of fellowship under the Old Testament, or the law, or the traditions of the church confessional.

Some teachers declare that sin committed by a Christian will produce a darkness of the mind and cite I John 1:6 as scriptural evidence.

I John 1:6 is teaching us that it isn't possible for an *unbeliever* to have fellowship with God because he is walking in darkness. For an unbeliever to say he has fellowship with God is a lie and he's not telling truth.

Believers are always in the light and always walk in the light. John 3:21 teaches that "those who do the truth come to the light." In John 8:12 Jesus said, "I am the light of the world, the one following me will *by no means walk in darkness* but will *have* the light of life." The light and life of

Christ are always together, to have one is to have the other. If we have the life of Christ we must also have the light of Christ. Someone may argue that according to John 8:12 if you're not following Christ you're not walking in the light. Jesus also said in John 10:27, "My sheep hear my voice, and I know them and *they follow me* and I give them eternal life and they shall by no means ever perish and no one shall sieze them out of my hand." All who are sheep hear this voice, follow, and have received everlasting life. There are no exceptions and there are no exclusions; they hear, they follow, they live and they walk in light!

Scripture after scripture teaches that the unsaved are in darkness and believers are in light. In Colossians 1:13, Paul teaches that the Father who made us fit for the inheritance of the saints of light transferred us from the power of darkness into the Kingdom of his beloved Son. In I Peter 2:9, the apostle Peter tells us we have been called out of darkness into his marvelous light. We cannot be transferred back and forth from the kingdom of light to the kingdom of darkness and back again after we confess our sins. There is no scripture that teaches this!

Having been transferred into the kingdom of light we always walk in the light. I John 1:7. Since "we walk in the light as he is in the light we have fellowship (i.e. with other true Christians) with each other and the blood of Jesus his Son cleanses us from *all* sin." Since all our sin is cleansed on the basis of an unchanging fellowship with Christ and his shed blood it's not possible for us to seek for forgiveness with a view to the cleansing of sin as many teach from I John 1:9.

The many scriptures that reveal the efficacy of the blood of Jesus Christ leave no doubt in the mind that cleansing of the believer's sin is absolute and complete and cannot be made conditional by the work of confession. Believers are unconditionally acquired, Acts 20:28, are justified,

Romans 5:9 are sealed, I Corinthians 11:25, are redeemed and forgiven, Ephesians 1:7, made nigh, Ephesians 2:13, redeemed and forgiven, Colossians 1:14, have peace, Colossians 1:20, redemption, Hebrews 13:12, are being sprinkled, I Peter 1:2, cleansed, I John 1:7, and have been washed from our sin, Revelation 1:5 by the blood of Jesus Christ and without *any* condition.

If we lost prayer fellowship with God because of a lack of confession we would be unable to pray for a restoration of fellowship!

Have we lost God's love? Romans 8:35-39 indicates His love pervades all obstacles. Have we lost forgiveness of sins? Where is the teaching of such condemnation for failure to confess? There are obviously many unanswered questions concerning this interpretation of I John 1:9.

If it is stated that the sin of I John 1:9 is Christian sin and that it is different than an unsaved person's sin where is the Scripture that teaches a differences in the quality of sin?

It becomes quite clear that the traditional teaching that confession of sin is necessary for the restoration of fellowship of the believer with God is a doctrine unsupported by the context of New Testament scripture and that to support such a concept Old Testament relationships between God and Israel must be used to describe a relationship between Christ and His church. We cannot return to the Hebrew altar for cleansing or to a concept of Hebrew priesthood for restoration of the presence and promises of God. We are unfailingly indwelt by the Spirit of God in an unbroken fellowship. "Reckon yourselves dead indeed unto sin and *alive* unto God," Romans 6:11.

The grammar of the passage of Scripture is perhaps as significant as the context of New Testament scripture in the interpretation of this passage of scripture.

First of all, the entire section from verses 6-10 of the

first chapter is made up of clauses of probability. These five verses contain five probability clauses which begin with the Greek particle, ean, in the subjunctive case. If the protasis is true then the apodosis is also probably true. In each case beginning at verse 6 the hypothesis of the protasis provides us with a true conclusion in the apodosis. (verse 6 protasis) "If we say we have fellowship with him and walk in darkness (verse 6 apodosis) "we lie and do not the truth." The explanation is that it is a lie to say we have fellowship with God when we walk in darkness. The unsaved walk in darkness but a Christian cannot walk in darkness. A Christian has been transferred from the Kingdom of darkness into the Kingdom of light. cf. II Corinthians 4:4-7, II Corinthians 6:14, Ephesians 5:8, Colossians 1:12, 13, I Thessalonians 5:5, I Peter 2:9. Even our Savior says in John 8:12, "He that followeth me shall not walk in darkness, but shall have the light of life." In John 10:27 Jesus says, "My sheep hear my voice, and I know them, and they follow me."

All Christians walk in light and since they all walk in light they all have fellowship with God. Therefore, according to the theme of I John walking in light is evidence of eternal life while walking in darkness is evidence of a lost condition.

The protasis of verse 7 is "If we walk in the light as he is in the light"; the apodosis is, "We have fellowship with each other and the blood of Jesus Christ his son, cleanses us from all sin." Here we have the evidence of eternal life in that walking in light produces fellowship with other Christians *and* absolute cleansing from sin. In verse 8, the *protasis* is "If we say that we have no sin"; the *apodosis* is "we deceive ourselves and the truth is not in us." Here, on the other hand, we have evidence that a person who professes to have no sin is obviously unsaved.

In verse 9, the protasis is, "If we confess our sins"; the apodosis is "He is faithful and righteous that he may forgive our sins and cleanse us from all iniquity." Here, again we have evidence of salvation; namely, that a saved person confesses or admits that he has sins both before becoming a Christian and also after becoming a Christian. All, then who really admit sin as opposed to those who will not admit sin receive the benefits of salvation which are the forgiving of the sins in our unsaved life plus the cleansing of iniquity from our Christian life.

In the 10th verse the protasis is, "If we say that we have not sinned"; the apodosis is "we make him a liar and his word is not in us." Obviously, here is evidence that a person is not a Christian who denies that he has sin. Thus, we have a parallelism of evidence for and against salvation. Hence, verse 9 is not instruction for sanctification or fellowship but evidence that one is really a Christian.

There is additional evidence that a comparison between the saved and unsaved is found in these verses in the two Greek words for "say" and "confess." The Greek word, eipo, is used to describe the lies of the unsaved and the Greek word, hom-o-log-e-o, is used to describe the truthful confession of a Christian. The Greek word, eipo, means to say something that may or may not be true while the Greek word, hom-o-log-e-o, is a speaking word that is in total agreement with the heart and soul of the individual and *"homogenous"* with the Christian's life.

Since the context and the grammar support the interpretation that I John 1:9 teaches a positive evidence of salvation and not a means of sanctification and since no other New Testament scripture teaches a sanctification by confession we must conclude the doctrine of maintenance of fellowship by confession is an erroneous tradition that has probably been retained as a form of the confessional. If you are willing to believe that Jesus paid it all; past, present, and future, even to the continuous sanctification of Christian life through His blood and priesthood, you will *really* be free to live for Him. John 8:32, "And ye shall know the truth, and the truth shall make you free." Praise the Lord!

Chapter 4

The Traditional Age of Accountability

As I mentioned in the introduction to this book, the salvation of infants and small children is an emotion-packed subject which has, in my opinion, a great amount of tradition incorporated in its' teaching.

The traditional teaching maintains that infants and small children are saved by a special mercy and grace of God up to an age when they become accountable for their sin. After this point, if they die without saving faith they are lost and go to hell.

There is a divergence of opinion as to what age children become accountable for their sins, but some suggest that the age is around the time of purberty or around fourteen years for boys and twelve years for girls.

One of the principle scriptures used to reinforce this tradition is II Samuel 12:23. After the death of David's child from an adulterous relationship with Bathsheba, David says, "But now he is dead, wherefore should I fast? Can I bring him back again? I shall go to him, but he shall not return to me."

Those who use this verse to support the tradition reason

that since David says, "I shall go to him," he is implying that the child will be in heaven when David meets him after David's death.

Another scripture that is used to support this tradition is I Corinthians 7:14 where Paul is encouraging a believing spouse to remain with an unbelieving spouse because the unbelieving spouse is sanctified by the believing spouse: "else were your children unclean; but now they are holy," he says.

Another possible scripture used to support this tradition is Acts 16:31 where Paul tells the Phillipian jailer, "Believe on the Lord Jesus Christ, and thou shall be saved, and thy house." They suggest that this verse teaches household salvation on the basis of the faith of a parent.

As I mentioned in the introduction when questioned as to my position on the salvation of infants, I can find no scripture that teaches a special grace from God for the salvation of infants.

The Scripture, in fact, goes to great lengths to teach that apart from a true faith in Jesus Christ as Lord and Savior all are lost. Ephesians 2:8 says we are saved "by grace through faith." Faith is a *necessity* for salvation. Faith involves the intellect and emotions of a person. In Acts 16:31 Paul tells us to *"believe"* on the Lord Jesus Christ and thou shall be saved." *Believing* is a *necessity* for salvation. Romans 3:10 declares "There is *none* righteous, no, *not one.*" Romans 3:23 teaches "For *all* have sinned and come short of the glory of God." In Psalm 51:5 David declares "Behold, I was shapen in iniquity; and in sin did my mother conceive me." John 3:36 declares "He that believeth on the Son hath everlasting life: and he that *believeth not* the Son shall not see life; but the wrath of God abideth on him."

Salvation depends on "faith" or "believing." *All* who do not or cannot believe do not possess eternal life.

"There is *none* righteous, no, not one." This includes Jews, Gentiles, old people, children, all people.

In the face of this clear teaching of the scripture concerning the lost condition of all people, and that righteousness and justification can only be received by believing in Jesus, the previously mentioned scriptures cannot support the doctrine of salvation of children by a special grace of God.

II Samuel 12:23, no doubt, means that David's son cannot return to the temporal world. He is now in a spiritual realm. David will, one day, also enter that spiritual realm.

I Corinthians 7:14 cannot be used to support the salvation of children because salvation is based on faith in Christ as Savior and Lord and not on family relationships or lineage. In John 8:39 the Jews testified that "Abraham is our father." This is true as far as physical lineage is concerned. Jesus answered, "If you were Abraham's children ye would do the works of Abraham." In other words, physical relationships can't save. Only spiritual relationships save. John 1:13 testifies the sons of God are those who "were born *not of blood,* nor of the will of the flesh, nor of the will of man, but of God."

I Corinthians 7:14 must be teaching that marriage in an unequal yoke is *not deterimental to the salvation* of the children. The opportunity for them to receive Christ as Savior and Lord is just as good in an unequal yoke as in a believer's equal yoke, therefore, the salvation of the children is no excuse to break up a marriage in an unequal yoke. If anything else is being taught here there is no reference to it in the rest of New Testament scripture that I can find. Certainly this scripture offers no evidence for a special method of salvation. To do so would be to contradict the mass of evidence supporting salvation by grace through faith only.

In the Acts 16:3 passage the misinterpretation of the verse is brought about by the phrase "and thy house." The word order translated by King James translators has suggested a special salvation for children because of a saved parent. Paul and Silas were preaching to the jailer and his family, cf. verse 32, when the jailer asked the question, "What must I do to be saved?" They answered, "Believe on the Lord Jesus and you and your household shall be saved." Each one of them believed and was baptized as a witness of their faith. Verse 34 tells us that all the household *believed God.* There is no salvation apart from *believing!*

At this point, with no hope for a special grace of salvation for infants and children there is a feeling of resentment toward God for seemingly condemning "innocent" infants to hell without an opportunity to be saved.

This same feeling could arise as one considers the countless thousands who have grown to maturity and have never heard the gospel. They haven't had a chance for salvation either! The mentally incompetant also haven't had a fair chance for salvation. Neither have those who have heard the gospel but haven't quite understood it had a fair chance for salvation. To solve this problem from a rationalistic point of view the only fair thing for God to do is to save everyone for even those who openly reject and curse God really don't know what they're doing. Jesus said it, himself, on the cross, Luke 23:34, "Father forgive them; for they know not what they do."

Universalism is not the answer to the problem. the scriptures are still true and there is "none righteous; no, not one." No matter what handicap they have for not believing the gospel unto salvation.

Deep within a Christian is the solemn conviction that even though I don't understand God and how he deals with mankind He still is faithful and true and I must believe Him and trust Him for the things I don't understand.

One of the interesting evidences of ultimate trust in God that this tradition of the "age of accountability" is not really believed by Christians is their attitude toward the present-day problem of abortion. Most Christians I know take a strong stand against abortion because, they maintain, it is murder. I agree. However, if we really believed that all children were saved up to the "age of accountability" we would have to soften our stand against it because all of the murdered infants are populating heaven. If they were allowed to grow up, many of them would reject Christ, but because of abortion they are saved and protected from losing their salvation!

The most dangerous thing about this tradition of the "age of accountability" is the failure of parents to take a serious role in the evangelization of their children. They assume that there will be a time when the children are older that they can seriously share the gospel of Christ with their children. Because of an untimely death many children have never had an opportunity to receive Christ because the parents felt they had time as long as the children were protected by the "special grace of God." Deuteronomy 6:7 makes it clear that God expects parents to teach their children the way of the Lord diligently.

Children are able to make a true decision for Christ as Savior and Lord at a very early age if they receive the proper training. Our daughter, Margaret, received the Lord at the age of three and recognizes her salvation beginning at this time.

But what can we do to ease the pain of the lost hope for children who have been unable to make a decision for Christ because they were too young to understand? We must reaffirm our trust in God that even though we can't understand his process of saving the lost, it is true and righteous altogether.

There is a verse of scripture that has helped me in this problem and perhaps will help you, also. In Revelation 20 verses 11-15 a description of the great white throne judgement is given. This is the judgement for the unsaved of all time. Verse 13 reads, "And the sea gave up the dead which were in it; and death and hell delivered up the dead which were in them; and they were judged every *according to their works.*" They were judged *according* to their works. The very wicked who have committed gross sin were judged *according* to their works. They will receive a severe judgement of great torment as the rich man of Luke 16:19 & 20 who withheld from the beggar at his gate. Then, also, they who have lived good lives will receive little torment or none, perhaps. God is just! God is fair! Infants who have committed no sin certainly will be excused from torment. But what about the awfulness of hell? How is it possible to escape the awful experience of hell? At the risk of starting a new tradition let me suggest how this might be. I have no scripture to justify this. I realize that it's dangerous to speculate, but because this tradition is so emotionally charged and is so contrary to the clear teaching of scripture let me pose a possibility that at least doesn't contradict scripture!

Jesus taught that in heaven there would be a great reward for faithfulness. In Matthew 25:14-30 "thou hast been faithful over a *few* things, I will make thee ruler over many things." In I Corinthians 3:12-15 Paul teaches that spiritual work will endure the fire of judgement. Therefore, the more of one's life lived "walking in the spirit" the more "reward" in heaven. It then is clear that greater and lesser reward will be received by those in heaven, and greater and lesser torment will be received by those in hell. Since God is perfectly fair and just and everyone will get exactly what he deserves there will, no doubt, be those in heaven, who because of lives wasted in fleshly living, will hardly experience any of the joy of heaven. As well, there will be those in hell who have committed no sin such as infants who will experience none of the torment of hell. A further thought concerning the destiny of people in heaven and hell is the stage of maturity at which people experience things.

There are repeated admonitions in the scriptures encouraging believers to mature in Christ. In I Corinthians 3:1 Paul calls the immature Christians "babes in Christ." cf. Hebrews 5:13, I Peter 2:2. Babies don't experience much of life. Their diet is "Pablum and Milk." Older people can enjoy "Steak and Lobster." Evidently, the capacity to enjoy heaven will be tied to "maturity." The immature experience or are aware of little that occurs around them. So it will be, I think, for some in heaven as well as some in hell. At any event, I know that God is just and the scriptures are true!

I would plead with Christian parents to win their children to Christ at a very early age. "The devil as a roaring lion, walketh about, seeking whom he may devour." I Peter 5:8. Don't let him devour your children.

Chapter 5

The Traditional Rescue From Hell

*T*he traditional rescue from hell, no doubt, began as part of a sixth century Gallican Creed.[1]

The traditional rescue from hell as described by Dr. Scofield in his reference Bible[2] and others teach that "hades was formerly in two division, the abodes respectively of the saved and of the lost." The tradition continues that after the ascension of Christ a change took place, in that, according to Ephesians 4:8-10, Jesus Christ, who himself, went to paradise after his death on the cross, took all of "paradise" with him when he ascended into heaven. Since Paul, also, experienced "paradise" when he was taken up to the third heaven and he calls this place "paradise" cf. II Corinthians 12:4, it is assumed that paradise was moved from hell to the third heaven by Jesus Christ at the ascension.

This tradition is based on the assumption that all of the

---

[1]Henry Bettenson, *Documents of the Christian Church,* (Oxford University Press, 1943), p. 347.

[2]Dr. C. I. Scofield, *The Scofield Reference Bible,* (Oxford University Press, New York, Inc., 1909, 1937), pp. 1098-99.

dead went down into hell into a two-compartment place for spirits and one compartment is called "paradise" and that the other compartment is called "hell." In the passage in Luke 16:19-31 there is no reference to "paradise" but only the statement that the "beggar died and was carried by the angels into Abraham's bosom; the rich man also died and was buried." Luke 16:22.

The tradition is probably reinforced by the idea that since the rich man could see Lazarous they were probably in the same place with a "great gulf fixed" between them which was some kind of a "grand canyon" through which there was little or no opportunity to cross. Luke 16:26.

Hell is always described in scripture as being *down*. cf. Deuteronomy 32:22, Job 11:8, Psalm 55:15, Psalm 86:13, Proverbs 9:18, Proverbs 15:24, Isaiah 14:9, 15, Ezekiel 31:16, Matthew 11:23, Luke 10:15, II Peter 2:4.

On the other hand, heaven is always described in scripture as being up. cf. Genesis 6:7, 7:19, 11:4, 22:11, 28:12, 49:25, etc.

It is also clear from scripture that none of the saints ever go *down* to hell; they always go *up* to heaven. cf. Genesis 5:24, II Kings 2:1,11, II Chronicles 18:18, Nehemiah 9:6, Jeremiah 33:22.

Therefore, even though it seems from the description of the position of the rich man in hell and the beggar in Luke 16, that they are in the same realm, the preponderance of evidence from scripture teaches that the beggar is in heaven where God dwells with Abraham and the rich man is in hell! It thus appears from this scripture that at least some of those who are in heaven can see some of those who are in hell and vice versa. It is also interesting to note from this passage of scripture in Luke 16 that the rich man in hell knew that he still had five living brothers on earth. cf verses 27-28. He must have been able to see earth as well as heaven.

Since the preponderance of scripture teaches that when

the faithful die they have always gone to heaven and when unbelievers die they go to hell, we need to take a more careful look at the scriptures that are used to support this tradition to discover the error of interpretation.

In Ephesians 4:8-10 the context of the passage of scripture begins with verse 7 and the giving of the gracious gifts of Christ. The giving of gifts then continues through verse 11 where the ministers to the church of Christ are listed. The verses in question are in the context of the gifts of Christ, so it is unlikely that Paul would change the subject and then go back to the subject he had originally begun with.

Verse 8 tells us "when he ascended up on high, he led captivity captive, and gave gifts to men." It was necessary for him to ascend on high before he could give gifts to men. In John 16:7 Jesus said, "It is expedient for you that I go away: for if I go not away, the Comforter will not come unto you: but, if I depart, I will send him unto you." The gracious gifts promised in Ephesians 4:7 are to be dispensed by the Holy Spirit, cf. John 16:13, "he will guide you into all truth." cf., also, I Corinthians 12:7-11, Romans 12:6, I Peter 4:10. The subject of the gracious gifts of Christ continues in verse 8 and we see why it was necessary, at least in part, for him to ascend to heaven. But what about leading captivity captive? What does this have to do with the gifts of Christ? His ascension on high completed the work of redemption for the redeemed through his death on the cross. His death on the cross paid the price for the forgiveness of sins for the lost who have faith in him, and his ascension on high makes application of the blood sacrifice for the cleansing of sin. Jesus Christ is *both* sins sacrifice and the high priest of God to make an offering of his own blood for the forgiveness of sins. Romans 4:25 says of Jesus Christ that it was he "who was delivered for our offenses, and was raised again for our justification. A sacrifice needs a living priest to offer it.

To whom are we captive? cf. II Timothy 2:26. Believers were captive to Satan before Jesus Christ ascended to be both sacrifice and high priest of the sacrifice of himself.

The concept of unbelievers being captive of Satan is well supported in scripture. Unbelievers cannot believe in Jesus Christ because Satan holds their mind captive. II Corinthians 4:4 declares "the god of this world hath blinded the minds of them which believe not, lest the light of the glorious gospel of Christ, who is the image of God, should shine unto them."

In II Timothy 2:26 Paul advises Timothy that by gentle, patient teaching there is a possibility that unbelievers might repent, "And that they may recover themselves out of the snare of the devil, who are taken captive by him at his will."

Other scriptures which teach the captivity of the unsaved to Satan are: Luke 4:18, John 8:32-44, I Peter 3:9, Isaiah 14:17, Isaiah 42:6-7, Isaiah 61:1.

This scripture in Ephesians 4:8 is teaching us that those who were held captive to Satan are now captives of Jesus Christ.

Paul considers himself a prisoner of Jesus Christ. cf. Ephesians 3:1, 4:1, Romans 1:1, I Corinthians 7:22. In reality all men are servants either to Satan or Jesus Christ. Paul testifies in Romans 6:16, "Know ye not, that to whom ye yield yourselves sevants to obey, his servants ye are to whom ye obey;"

A question that might arise from this scripture is "Why was it necessary for Jesus to ascend to liberate Satan's captives?" The answer is that the process of redemption wasn't complete until sin's sacrifice on Calvary's cross was offered by God's priest at the right hand of the Father. Hebrews 1:3 tells us "when he had by himself purged our sins, sat down at the right hand of the Majesty on high;" His being seated signified the completion of his work. cf. Hebrews 9:12.

"Nor through the blood of goats and of calves but through His own blood *he entered once for all* into the holies, having found eternal redemption." His ascension made it possible to free those to whom redemption was promised by a completed work of redemption. His ascension also made it possible for him to bestow the gifts of the Spirit on the redeemed on earth.

The ninth verse teaches us that this redemptive work of Jesus Christ would not have been possible without his descent to the earth that he might die on the cross for man's sin and then be buried in the earth and rise again the third day according to His prophecy.

Some have suggested that his descent into the "lower parts" of the earth indicates that he spiritually descended into hell. To support this idea they use Acts 2:27 which says, "Because thou wilt not leave my soul in hell, neither wilt thou suffer thine Holy One to see corruption." This scripture is speaking of the *body* of Jesus Christ and not his spirit. It is not possible that the spirit of Jesus Christ could be corrupted because he is God, but it could have been possible for the body of Jesus Christ to be corrupted if it had lain in the grave for a longer period of time than three days. The expression "my soul in hell" in the 27th verse is speaking of his human awareness joined to corporiality. Christ never lost human or divine awareness but he lost the corporial experience of human awareness because his body was in a grave for three days. Also, lest there be any confusion about what is meant by the expression, "my soul in hell" in verse 27, it is made clear in verse 31 where Peter explains that David was prophesying the *resurrection* of Jesus Christ. *Resurrection* pertains only to the body, not the spirit.

The next question that might be asked is, "What happened to the spirit of Jesus Christ while his body was in the grave for three days?"

There are two scriptures which tell us where his spirit was while his body remained in the grave.

The first scripture to be considered is Luke 23:46. As Jesus was releasing his spirit from his body on Calvary's cross he cried, "Father, into thy hands I commit my spirit." There is no scripture that teaches that when the Father received the spirit of Christ into his hands he sent it to hell. There was no purpose for such an act. On the contrary, there was a restoration of trinity fellowship similar to that which had been expreienced before the incarnation.

This second scripture which describes where Jesus' spirit was during the time his body was in the grave seems to me to be even more persuasive.

In John 17:1-5, Jesus prays to his Father just before he is going to the cross. He tells the Father that he has completed the work which he was given to do on earth. Then He requests that there might be a restoration of pre-creation trinitarian glory in verse 5. He prays, "And now, O Father, glorify thou me with thine own self with the glory *which I had with thee before the world was.*" His spirit was with the Father while his body lay in the grave. His prayer was answered and he for those three days that his body lay in the grave experienced the pre-creation trinitarian glory he had known in eternity past.

Psalm 68:18 from which Ephesians 4:8 is quoted is a "Victory" Psalm. The greatest victory the world has ever known is Jesus Christ rising from the grave and presenting the blood of the everlasting covenant before the Father for the redemption of the world. Praise the Lord!

A final scripture to be considered which is often used to support the idea of a two-compartment hell from which Christ delivers the faithful is I Peter 3:19. This verse says, "By which also he went and preached unto the spirits in prison:" Here, again, *traditional* teaching has been substituted for the *truth* of the word because of a failure to grasp the context of the passage of scripture. The theme of the epistle of I Peter is Christians suffering. I Peter 3:19 is in the context of "suffering for well doing." cf. 3:17, 4:1. It would be inappropriate to bring up the subject of the gifts of Christ in the midst of an explanation of how to suffer for "well doing."

Verse 18 is teaching us that Christ once suffered for "well doing" by being "put to death in the flesh but quickened in the Spirit:"

Verse 19 is teaching that this same living spirit of Christ preached to "spirits in prison."

It is verse 20 which makes it clear that this verse cannot support the traditional rescue of saints from a two-compartment hell. Verse 20 says these "spirits in prison" were "disobedient." It also says they were disobedient during the time while Noah was building the Ark. This is an exclusive *time segmented* group of *unbelievers* to whom Christ's spirit is preaching through Noah's ministry for God. This fits the concept of suffering for "well doing." Noah is doing good by building an ark and warning the disobedient of the coming flood, but unbelievers are ridiculing him for even supposing there could be a flood or even enough water to float an ark. They are called "spirits in prison" because they are, first of all, the prisoners of Satan and secondly, they are "spirits in prison" because they are confined outside the ark, in fact, imprisoned on "death row" with no hope of pardon unless they repent.

Verse 21 continues the subject of suffering for "well doing" by explaining that those eight souls who suffered for "well doing" and *through faith* enter the ark for safekeeping from the flood are like those who by faith are separated from the unbelievers by baptism and often endure the ridicule of unbelievers for their testimony of faith. cf. I Peter 4:4. Like the eight in Noah's day who endured ridicule and were spared from judgement, so those who endure ridicule for their faith in our time will be spared from judgement.

If the wider context of scripture had been consulted in Luke 16:26, Acts 2:27, Ephesians 4:8, and I Peter 3:19 the traditional teaching of "Christ's rescue from hell" would not have arisen.

Chapter 6

The Tradition of Speaking in Tongues

Since the doctrine of speaking in tongues is well established in the scripture shouldn't it be considered *truth* rather than *tradition*? Because a doctrine is found in scripture doesn't necessarily make it truth for our time. For instance, the brazen altar on which animal sacrifices were burned is a part of the Old Testament doctrine of atonement, but we do not carry the brazen altar into New Testament worship. The doctrine of tongues is a New Testament doctrine, however, so shouldn't it be a part of the New Testament church? Just as the brazen altar is no longer part of our worship, so it is that much doctrine found in the New Testament is no longer applicable to New Testament worship. We no longer have the priest's office, Luke 1:9, the laws of purification, Luke 2:22, the "law," Luke 2:39 and the passover supper, Luke 22:1. All these doctrines are in the New Testament but they aren't a part of church life. A doctrine becomes obsolete when it is made so by a statement of scripture. Hebrews 7 teaches the termination of the Levitical priesthood. Hebrews 8 teaches the termination of the Old Testament and Hebrews 10 teaches the termination of the Old Testament sacrifices. To follow or obey these doctrines today would be to follow *tradition* rather than the *truth.*

I believe the doctrine of speaking in tongues is terminated by the same means.

I Corinthians 13:8 without any question teaches that tongues *will cease.* At the time that Paul is writing this letter to the Corinthians the gift of tongues is still operative in the churches. Therefore, Chapters 13 and 14 are written to explain the proper use of the gift. Some have reasoned that since the instructions on the use of the gift is found in such detail, that the gift must be in effect in the churches in our time. This would be true, if it weren't for the specific explanation that as verse 10 declares, "But when that which is perfect come, then *that which is in part shall be done away."*

That which is in part is that described in verse 9, "For we know in part, and we prophecy in part."

The question as to how "prophecies shall fail, tongues shall cease, and knowledge shall vanish away" as found in verse 8 is difficult to answer. To make it even more difficult the original Greek language says, "Prophecies will be abolished." What will happen to the prophecies and knowledge? How will the prophecies of scripture be done away with? How will knowledge be done away with? Certainly prophecies and knowledge will continue, but not in their *partial manifestations.* This is exactly what verses 9 and 10 say. Incomplete prophecies and incomplete knowledge must be abolished in favor of *complete prophecies* and *complete knowledge.* Will there ever be a time when the church has *complete knowledge* and *prophecy?* Paul says this will be when *"that which is perfect is come."* Partial knowledge, prophecy, and tongues will no longer be in the church when that which is *"perfect"* is come.

There are very few things that are perfect in the sense

in which we think of perfection. God is perfect, the three persons of the Godhead are perfect, and some have suggested that when the church is raptured it will be perfect. Since both Jesus Christ and the Holy Spirit had already come this scripture cannot be referring to God. Otherwise, the scripture would have said, "When that which is perfect is come, *again,* then that which is in part shall be done away." But it doesn't say that! It say, "When that which is perfect has come, *then* that which is in part shall be done away."

To interpret "that which is perfect" as the church is closer to a logical interpretation of the scripture. When the church is raised into the presence of the Lord all sin in the flesh will be gone from its' membership and the environment will be Holy. This also would allow for the gift of tongues and knowledge and prophecy in partial expressions.

I do not believe "that which is perfect" is the church when it is raised to be with Christ. Let me give you my reasons:

1. The Greek word for perfect is "telos." It can be properly translated "perfect thing" thus giving emphasis to the fact that the word possesses neuter gender. In the Greek language the word for church "ekklesia" is of the feminine gender. If the church were in Paul's mind he would have used the feminine gender instead of neuter gender. He, also, could have simply said, "When the church is raised then that which is in part shall be done away."

2. The broad context of this passage of scripture includes chapters 12-14 and in the widest context is a teaching on the gifts of the Spirit. Chapter 12 enumerates the gifts of the Spirit and explains their use in the church should benefit the church. Each member has a special gift of the Spirit, a special place in the church and should not seek a place or gift that has not been given by the Holy Spirit.

Chapter 13 begins with the first words of correction for the misuse of the gift of tongues in the Corinthian Church.

Although several gifts of the Spirit are named in verses 28-31 of Chapter 12 only the speaking gifts are singled out for correction in Chapters 13 and 14.

Therefore the context of this passage of scripture has narrowed to the speaking gifts.

Paul's first point of correction for the use of the speaking gifts is that they are not being exercised in love. It is for this reason that some have inappropriately called Chapter 13 the "love chapter." It is really the tongues chapter, for that is its context. Tongues, to be fruitfully used under the ministry of the Holy Spirit, must be exercised in love. They are worthless without love. The evidence that tongues are not being exercised in love is suggested in the questions of 12:30, "Do all speak in tongues? Do all interpret?" Evidently, many were seeking a gift that the Spirit had given to only a few.

A second evidence for the misuse of tongues is for personal enjoyment or edification. In chapter 14:12 Paul's second rebuke is his exhortation to "seek that ye may excel to the edifying of the church." If there had been love in the exercise of the gift neither of these problems would have arisen. They wouldn't have sought for or expressed a gift for their personal glory. cf. verse 4, "Charity envieth not; charity vaunteth not itself, is not puffed up." Verse 5, "Seeketh not her own."

The point I want to make is that the church is not in the context of the scripture in Chapter 13. The subject is: *"The speaking gifts should be expressed in love."* It is not logical for Paul to interject a thought of the church when he is trying to persuade the Corinthian Church to express the speaking gifts in love.

It is for this reason that the "church" is not "that which is perfect" in this passage of scripture.

The only logical, contextual, interpretation for "that which is perfect" is "the New Testament." By this I mean the complete canon of the New Testament scriptures.

At A.D. 59, the suggested date of writing of the epistle of I Corinthians, only a small percentage of the New Testament had been committed to writing. For twenty years after the resurrection of Jesus Christ, the church depended on memory and a verbal sharing of the gospel. This time in church history is known as the period of the "oral gospel." As letters to the churches were written by Paul and others a catalog of scriptures began to be collected and preserved and copied for the use of the churches. The New Testament is the collection of these gospels and epistles. That period of revelation was terminated at about 100 A.D. in the completed New Testament canon of scriptures. That which is perfect is the completed canon of the New Testament scriptures. Here are the reasons why I believe this is the proper interpretation:

1. God's word is called "perfect" in Psalm 19:7. In II Timothy 3:17, God's word produces perfection in those who are admonished by it.

2. The context of I Corinthians 13 is the speaking gifts. Hence, prophecy or the word of God is the central theme of the chapter.

3. "Perfect thing" is an appropriate translation for the Greek word, "telion," translated "perfect," in the King James Bible.

4. A definition of the Greek word, "telion" is "brought to completion, fully accomplished, fully developed."[1]

5. I Corinthians 13:11 agrees with the concept of an incomplete canon of scriptures which will one day be complete and can be called "perfect."

A child only has the partial understanding of an adult so Paul says, "When I was a child, I spake as a child, I understood as a child, I thought as a child." The church of

---

[1] *The Analytical Greek Lexicon* (Harper & Brothers, New York), p. 400

Jesus Christ was immature in its understanding at the time that Paul is writing this letter. Paul, himself, has much to learn, and much he will never have the opportunity of knowing because his life will end before the New Testament is complete. However, Jesus Christ has revealed to him the fact that a time will come when the church will have the complete revelation of God for its use. When that time comes, as a mature body it will "put away childish things."

Partial knowledge will be replaced by a full knowledge, partial prophecies will be replaced by a complete prophecy, tongues will cease.

6. I Corinthians 13:12 also agrees with the concept of an incomplete canon of scriptures in which it is difficult to see the "face of God" at the time that Paul is writing this letter, but he is confident that "when that which is perfect is come" he will be able to see clearly as "face to face."

He then reiterates the concept of a partial revelation of the Word of God as he says, "Now I know in part; but then shall I know even as also I am known." He never arrived at this ultimate knowledge while on earth, but I'm sure he's experiencing it now in the presence of the Lord.

I'm sure for most of us this is true. Even though we have a complete revelation of God through his word there is much more to appreciate in His presence.

7. It seems to me the Holy Spirit has confirmed this interpretation of I Corinthians 13:12 by a reference to looking through a glass in two other New Testament scriptures.

Apart from the references to glass in the book of Revelation, I Corinthians 13:, II Corinthians 3:18 and James 1:23 are the only New Testament reference to glass. The references in the book of Revelation all relate to the vision John saw of the heavenly city, Jerusalem. The floors and the city, itself, appeared to be made of glass. The previously mentioned scriptures, however, all relate to the word of God, thus, producing a larger context of evidence that "That which is perfect" is the New Testament canon.

Some commentators have indicated glass was not made during New Testament times, but that the references to glass in the New Testament refer to metal mirrors. I was pleased to discover, while visiting the Smithsonian Institution in Washington, D.C., that they are wrong. They have glass on display contemporary with New Testament times.

It is true, however, that the glass I saw was of a poor transparency, so it is an added evidence that Paul's description of looking "through a glass darkly" fits the nature of the product contemporary with his writing.

Paul's description of "through a glass darkly."

There are two Greek words for glass in the New Testament. The word used in Revelation is "haylo." John's description of this glass is one of semi-transparency and golden in color. It is a "contruction material" for the floors and the city, itself. cf. Revelation 21:18. The word is derived from the Greek word for jacinth.

A word of explanation should be made concerning the word, "esoptron" which has been translated "glass" by the King James translation and which I, also, have translated as "glass." Most modern language translations have translated this word, "mirror" on the basis of lexical definitions arrived at by word usage contemporary with the writing of the epistle.

Once again, the argument for interpretation should rest more strongly on context than on history, in my opinion.

I have previously made the statement that the Greek word used for "glass" in King James and "mirror" in modern language translations "esoptron" is made of two Greek words "eis" a Greek preposition meaning "into" and the Greek word "horao" which means "to see." The source for this statement is the Greek-English Analytical Concordance of the Greek-English New Testament by J. Stengina, 1963. This book is published by Hellenes-English Biblical Foundation, P. O. Box 10412, Jackson 9, Miss., U.S.A. I am quoting information found on page 574 I.F. 3.

On this same page Stengina, in addition to giving the root source for "esoptron" in I Corinthians 12:13 and James 1:23, gives the root source for the word glass used in II Corinthians 3:18 as "kata," a Greek preposition meaning along or beside and "harao" which means "to see."

The conclusion one might arrive at from the root source of these words is that in I Corinthians 13:12 and James 1:23 the root source clearly teaches the concept of "seeing into" while the II Corinthians 3:18 passage teaches to see along or beside thus suggesting the concept of reflection or a mirror. Since, however, both I Corinthians 13:12 and James 1:23-25 suggest to effectively see Christ in the Word one must use God's Word as a window rather than a mirror the II Corinthians 3:18 passage to effectively change a person from "glory to glory" must also infer the use of the word as a window rather than a mirror.

The root meaning of the words used in all three passages of scripture then forms the first argument for a definitional context of interpretation of these three texts.

The second argument for interpretation of these three texts is the context of the grammar in I Corinthians 13:12. Paul says literally "For yet we see *through* a glass in obscurity." He does not say we see *in* a glass or *upon* a glass or *along* a glass or even *into* a glass but *through* a glass. If he had chosen any other Greek preposition other than "dia" we might conceed he was speaking of the use of a mirror in this verse. It is not possible, however, to see *through* a mirror. Any mirror that can be seen through is not a mirror in the true sense of the word but a glass or window used *as* a mirror.

The third contextual argument for the interpretation of

these three passages of scripture is that each passage of scripture describes some hinderance to seeing the holiness of God. In I Corinthians 13:12, Paul would be able to see the holiness of God "face to face" were it not for the obscurity produced by the incomplete "knowledge" and "prophecy" at the time he is writing his letter to the Corinthian Church. He reminds his readers, however, that love will compensate for an effective use of the gifts until a clearer, more definitive description of Christ's presence in the Church is revealed by the completion of New Testament Scriptures.

In II Corinthians 3:18 the hinderances to seeing the holiness of God is the veil that Moses put over his face (cf. II Corinthians 3:13) because of God's glory that was emanating from his face after having been with God. Other hinderances to seeing the glory and holiness of God is the blindness God placed upon Israel, II Corinthians 3:14-15. There is the promise, however, that God will one day remove this veil from Israel (cf. II Corinthians 3:16). However, for New Testament Christians, even though there may be some obscurity, the glory of the Lord is revealed in the Word and each time a Christian sees the glory of the Lord in the Word he experiences a metamorphasis or transformation to the image of Christ.

The third hinderance to seeing the glory and holiness of the Lord in the Word is the attitude of the reader of the Scriptures in James 1:23-25.

The emphasis that James is making beginning with James 1:21 is that if God's Word is read with a meek spirit it will save the soul, but if it is read with filthiness and superfluity of evil the word will not be implanted in the heart and mind.

One who reads God's Word with filthiness or superfluity of evil is like a man who views himself in a glass and forgets what he looked like. It did him no good to look at himself in the reflection of the glass for he forgot what he looked like. He remained unchanged as a result of this experience. He is a hearer of the Word but not a doer of the Word. His attitude of filthiness kept him from receiving any good from the Word.

On the other hand, one who looks into the perfect law of freedom and retains it because of a meek attitude becomes one who expresses his faith by his works and will be blessed and changed as a result of his experience. Thus, for the egocentric the Word of God is used like a person seeing his reflection in a window. However, for the meek the Word of God becomes a window through which he can see the glory of the Lord and is changed into the image of the Lord by the experience.

In II Corinthians 13:12 Paul is telling us that at the time he is writing to the Corinthian Church the combined partial prophetic gifts of the Spirit are presenting an obscured vision of the revelation of God. He is insisting that the virtue of love, however, will compensate for both the understanding and the expression of the partial prophetic gifts of the spirit.

In II Corinthians 3:18 the revelation of God is again in view as Paul writes to the Corinthians concerning the life-changing power of the word of God.

He illustrates the power of God's word by its affect on Moses, II Corinthians chapter 3, verses 6-13, in that his face shone so brilliantly after his communion with God that he had to wear a veil over his face so he wouldn't frighten the Israelites. cf. Exodus 34:33.

The New Testament also has the glory of God within its' context. cf. II Corinthians 3:11.

Verse 8 teaches us that since we have no veil over God's glory in the word as Moses had over his face, the affect of looking into or "upon" the word changes us into the image of the glory of Christ. This image-changing power occurs every time we assimilate New Testament truth by the power of the Holy Spirit.

In James 1:23 the word of God is once again in view as we are warned against an improper use of God's word. A window may be used in two ways. One may look through it to see things on the other side or one may concentrate on his reflection in the glass. This reflective property of glass is especially effective if the glass is slightly obscured. It is easier to see yourself in it if it is harder to see through it. This is, no doubt, what James has in mind as he warns against using God's word as a "mirror" to see only one's personal glory.

When one uses God's word to see God's glory he is changed, and the change produces an obedience to God and a change in his lifestyle. cf. Isaiah 6:5.

Thus, it seems to me, the Holy Spirit has tied these three references together to illustrate with "glass" the experience of seeing God in his word. Perhaps it was Paul's experience of being taken up to the third heaven, or his communion with Christ in the desert of Arabia that made him sense the imperfect image of God in the partial revelations of his time. At any rate, this final agreement of context in I Corinthians 13 strengthens the interpretation that that which is "perfect" is the completed canon of New Testament scripture.

"Tradition" teaches that some of the gifts of the Holy Spirit are in the church today that the "truth" teaches became obsolete with the completion of the New Testament. It is no surprise, then, that scriptures written after I Corinthians have little or no reference to the gift of tongues. Its' purpose as a sign to the Jews was no longer necessary because of the outstanding witness to the Jews by the Holy Spirit at Pentacost and during the period of the "oral gospel." After this period the gospel was spread mostly to the Gentile nations. It's purpose as a revealer of prophecy to individuals who, in turn, would share it in the church diminished as a substantial percentage of New Testament scriptures began circulating among the churches and finally, ceased by the completion of the New Testament at about 100 A.D.

One might reason that you can't argue against the experience of tongues in the church today. That is certainly true! They are being experienced by many serious, devout Christians. It is also true that many serious and devout Christians are experiencing "blessing" who adhere to other traditions in the church, but experience is not the final authority for Christian conduct. God's word is the final and only authority for faith and practice. To favor experience over truth is to turn one's back to God's glory. "All scripture is given by inspiration of God, and is profitable for *doctrine*, for *reproof*, for *correction*, for instruction in *righteousness:* that the man of God may be perfect, thoroughly furnished unto all good works" II Timothy 3:16-17. cf. II Corinthians 3:18, James 1:23-25.

Special miracles were produced by our Lord and the apostles for very special purposes. Jesus walked on water and raised the dead. He healed many people during his ministry and many of the miracles were recorded in the New Testament for our benefit. John 20:30-31 says, "And many other signs truly did Jesus in the presence of his disciples, which are not written in this book: But these are written, that ye might believe that Jesus is the Christ, the son of God; and that believing ye might have life through his name." In other words, the miracles of Jesus Christ provided proof that he was the *Son of God* so that we might have faith in him for salvation. If another would come who could duplicate the miracles of Christ we might be tempted to discredit the miracles of Christ as being an exceptional display of God's approval on his son. If anyone could exceed the miracles of Christ men would rather believe in him than Christ. It seems a dangerous thing to me to attempt to duplicate the miracles of Christ because it seems to me we would rob Him of His glory. Also, Jesus, himself, said in Luke 11:29, "This is an evil generation; they seek a sign;" Although this was said of the Jews who did not have the indwelling presence of the Holy Spirit it is, no doubt, even more applicable to those who possess the Holy Spirit. cf. I Corinthians 1:22, I Corinthians 14:22.

One may reason that the apostles also performed miracles, so didn't they rob the glory from Jesus by the miracles they performed? In II Corinthians 12:12 Paul testifies of the unusual miracles he performed which he calls "the signs of an apostle." Also, in Hebrews 2:4 those that "heard" Christ and spoke his word were able to perform unusual miracles. The reason for the miracles is also given in verses 3 and 4. They performed unusual apostolic miracles so that those who heard them speak the word of the Lord would reverence His word and believe it.

These miracles were numerous during the period of the "oral gospel." However, as the canon of New Testament scriptures was completed the authority transferred from the speakers to the written word. The question asked by the writer of Hebrews in 64 A.D. is also appropriate for today's church. Verse 53, "How shall we escape if we neglect so great salvation; which at the first began to be *spoken by the Lord?*" The *truth* is the Word of God!

Chapter 7

The Christmas Tradition

*D*ecember 25 has long been accepted as the birthdate of Jesus. However, there is good evidence from Scripture that the birth of Christ actually occurred in late spring.

The account of the conception of Jesus Christ found in Luke's Gospel presents the best information for arriving at the month of his birth.

Here are the facts presented in this passage:

Luke 1:25 tells us that it was in the sixth month that the angel Gabriel was sent to Mary. The sixth month of the Jewish calendar is the same as our ninth month or the month of September. The evidence for this is found in Exodus 12:2 where the Lord said to Moses "this month shall be unto you the beginning of months; it shall be the first month of the year to you." Dr. Scofield in his center column reference refers to this month as April. Exodus 13:4 calls this month the month of Abib. The Hebrew people faithfully celebrated the passover on the first month of their year through their generations and the passover month has become for Christians a celebration of the death, burial, and resurrection of Christ which occurs at the same time of the year as passover.

If we assume a 9-month human gestation period for the birth of Jesus Christ then nine months from the conception of Jesus Christ in September would place the birth in June.

It appears from the scriptural account of the appearance of the angel to Mary that conception occurred at this Jewish sixth-month appearance. The scriptural account places the conception of Christ between verses 35 and 36 of Luke, chapter 1. Verse 35 refers to the conception of Christ as a future event in these words. "The Holy Ghost *shall* come upon thee and the power of the Highest *shall* overshadow thee; therefore, also, that Holy Thing which shall be born of thee be called the Son of God."

Luke 1:36 refers to the conception of Jesus Christ as a past event in these words. "And, behold, thy cousin, Elizabeth, *she hath also conceived a son* in her old age and this is the sixth month with her, who was called barren. Mary is included with Elizabeth as one who has conceived. Elizabeth at this time was in her sixth month of gestation and would deliver in three more months or the month of December. December is John the Baptist's birth month and June is the birth month of Jesus Christ.

The month of June is shown to be the month of the birth of Christ by the circumstantial evidence of the activities of the people. Bethlehem is a town in the northern hemisphere and is evidently subject to similar weather conditions as are experienced in the northern half of the United States. Cold temperatures and occasional snow is not the best time to be grazing sheep as given in the December 25th, traditional date, of the birth of Christ.

Luke 2:8 tells us that in the same country, that is of Bethlehem, there were shepherds abiding in the field, keeping watch over their flocks by night.

Spring grass has now begun to grow and the shepherds are sleeping with their flocks in the open pastures taking advantage of the new food supply and warmer weather for their pastoral pilgrimage. During the colder weather the sheep were, no doubt, kept in shelters and fed hay as in our country. It certainly would not seem prudent to be guarding sheep in the open cold weather of December.

Since the Scripture gives such good evidence for a June birth for Jesus Christ shouldn't we try to change Christmas to June? That is probably not possible. Tradition is much stronger than scripture and we can't change the traditional values of the world and Christendom, but we can, when we have the opportunity, teach the truth of Scripture. We are reminded of a well-meaning businessman, opposed to religious practices, who said, "The next thing these fundamental Christians will try to do is put Christ in Xmas!"

Another of the interesting traditional teachings of the birth of Christ is that "three wise men came from the east and gave gifts to the newborn infant."

I can remember as a boy taking part in a Christmas drama in which I played the part of a wise man and came and bowed before the baby Jesus and gave him my Christmas wrapped gift of gold while singing, "We Three Kings." This traditional concept of the Christmas story will, no doubt, be repeated this next December by well-meaning evangelical Christians, thus perpetuating erroneous traditions which oppose the truth of Scripture.

Someone assumed that there were three wise men since there were three kinds of gifts offered to Christ. There is no Scripture that tells is how many wise men there were. There could have been two or twenty.

In Matthew 2:1 an unfortunate time concept is translated, "Now *when* Jesus was born in Bethlehem of Judea in the days of Herod the king, behold, there came wise men from the east to Jerusalem." Thus, the implication of this translation suggests that the wise men appeared at his birth.

However, a literal translation of this verse is: "Now Jesus having been born in Bethlehem of Judea in the days of Herod the King, behold, Magi from the east arrived in Jerusalem." It must have been Matthew's intention to differentiate this Jesus from others by saying "the one having been born in Bethlehem of Judea" rather than suggest a time element for the appearance of the wise men.

Jesus must have been about eighteen months old when the wise men visited him, for Matthew 2:7 tells us, that Herod inquired of them the time when the star first appeared. Then, on the basis of this information, he ordered all children under the age of two years old to be slain. cf. Matthew 2:16. He, no doubt, needed a safety factor to be sure he had eliminated the heir-apparent to the throne but about six months rather than two years would have been a sufficiently safe margin of error if Christ had just then been born.

Other internal evidence in this passage points to the concept that the Christ child must have been about eighteen months old for he is called a *"young child"* in verses 13, 14, literally, "the child," "pais," while at the birth of Christ in Luke 1:12 Jesus is called a *"babe,"* "brephos."

Another interesting possibility for interpretation is the position of the Magi in viewing the star. Matthew 2:1 tells us "Magi from the east arrived in Jerusalem." In other words eastern Magi had sighted the "Kings star" approximately eighteen months before they interviewed Herod concerning his birth. Matthew 2:2, however, presents a puzzling concept for it quotes the Magi as saying, "we have seen His star in the east." If this is meant as the direction they looked to see the star then they were west of the star to be able to see the star "in the east." But if this verse means we have seen his star *while* in the east the Scriptures don't say so. cf. also verse 9. Were they attending an astronomer's convention somewhere on the coast of the Mediterranian Sea when they first discovered the star? What delayed their coming? Was it distance or circumstances? We will probably not be able to find answers for these questions but it poses some interesting speculation.

Some more interesting speculation arises over the guidance of the star for the Magi. Remember that Herod expects to find Jesus in Bethlehem but Joseph and Mary were only there to pay their taxes. Their hometown was Nazareth. It appears from the Scripture that the King Star led the wise men in an easterly direction to Jerusalem and that having conversed with Herod were told to head south to Bethehem to find the child. However, the evening after their talk with Herod, they saw the star not in the south where Herod had instructed them to go, but northward toward Nazareth. The star continued to move in a northward direction until it settled over the carpenter's home of Joseph of Nazareth. It was here they found the approximately eighteen-month-old child to whom they presented their gifts.

It's also interesting to note that the trip to Egypt was not as often pictured with Joseph leading a donkey upon which Mary is riding with a new-born infant but the parents are traveling with an approximately eighteen-month-old boy to the land of Egypt.

A more scriptural Christmas tradition would go something like this:

On the night that Jesus was born in Bethlehem there was a faint fragrance of early spring flowers drifting through the night air as the shepherds slept in the doors of their rock-fenced sheep folds. The contented sheep were chewing their cuds and the night was brilliantly illuminated with stars and quiet except for the occasional bleating of a spring lamb or sheep.

The shepherds were suddenly awakened by a brilliant light shining on their camp! Even more startling was the appearance of a semi-transparent man in the midst of the illumination who spoke to them and said, "Don't be afraid,

for behold, I announce to you a great joy which shall be to
all the people, because today there was born to you in
David's City a Savior, who is Christ, the Lord." "And this
shall be evidence to you in that you will find a baby wrapped
in blankets and lying in a manger."

The shepherds already overwhelmed with the presence
and message of the angel were even more awe-struck by the
appearance of thousands of the heavenly angelic army
praising God and saying, "Glory to God in the heavens and
on earth peace to men of good will."

After the appearance of the angels the sky returned to
its somber black, studded with bright stars and the shepherds
decided to go to Bethlehem and see for themselves this
event which the Lord had made known to them.

Hurrying along they came and found Mary and Joseph
and in the manger, the baby, Jesus. From that time on they
told everyone about what had happened to them and of the
prophecy concerning his ministry as Savior and his title,
"Christ the Lord." Everyone became excited by the shepherds evangel. The shepherds, themselves, continued to
praise and glorify God for the things which they had seen
and heard.

Eight days after the birth of Christ he was circumcised
according to Jewish law and officially named, "Jesus."

After another thirty-three days, according to the Hebrew purification rite for women giving birth, Joseph and
Mary brought Jesus to Jerusalem to present him to the
Lord, according to the regulations for the firstborn and to
offer the proper sacrifices.

It was at this occasion that Simeon, to whom the Holy
Spirit had prophesied that he would not die until he had seen
Christ, the Lord, saw the Christ, took him in his arms and
blest him. He then prayed that he might die in peace because
he had seen God's salvation in Jesus Christ. Simeon also
blessed Mary and Joseph and prophesied concerning Christ.

Anna, a prophetess, came in while Simeon was giving his blessing and making prophesies concerning Christ. She then carried the good news to all who were looking for this redemption in Jerusalem.

After these things, Mary, Joseph and Jesus returned to Nazareth and Jesus became a toddler of about eighteen months when a caravan of men came to Nazareth. They were eastern astrologers who were calling attention to an unusual star they had been tracking which had come to reside over Nazareth. They said they had visited Jerusalem and in the process of tracking the "King star" and had been told by Herod and his priests that Christ was to be born in Bethlehem. Herod had even given them instructions to go to Bethlehem and worship Christ and then to return and tell him the address so that he could also go and worship the Christ.

This, however, was just a ploy, because he wanted the address and age of the child so that he might kill him.

The astrologers continued the account of their star trek by saying they were surprised to discover that the star they had been following didn't move south toward Bethlehem as Herod had informed them but northward to the city of Nazareth and, in fact, had come to rest over the house of Joseph the carpenter.

After they had come in the house they fell down and worshipped the young boy and presented him with gifts of gold, frankincense and myrrh.

That evening after the astrologers had retired they were awakened by a dream in which God warned them not to tell Herod that they had found Christ in Nazareth and that they should not take the main roads on their way home.

The next evening Joseph was awakened by the appearance of an angel in a dream telling him to flee from Nazareth to Egypt so that Herod would not be able to find the Christ child and kill him.

The next morning Mary and Joseph quickly packed and took Jesus and traveled to Egypt where they lived until Herod had died. They were then able to return to Nazareth where the Scripture of the prophets was fulfilled, "He shall be called a Nazarene."

Chapter 8

We're Saints – Not Sinners

*H*ave you ever heard some well meaning Christian say, "we're just sinners saved by grace?" They then glow with pride as they excuse themselves for their failure in achieving in the Christian life. Such apology for failure is a discouragement not only to the one giving the testimony but to those who must listen to it. All Christians want more from the Christian experience than the commentary of an experience basically unchanged from the unsaved experience of life.

We have memorized II Corinthians 5:17, "therefore if any man be in Christ, he is a new creature:" but very little seems new. "All things" really are not new and discouragement is not long in coming to the one who had such high hopes for a different exciting life in Christ.

Part of the problem is an identity crisis. We were a sinner before we were saved and according to well-meaning Christian friends we still are sinners but with this distinction that we are saved by grace. One must just have faith, that having said the magic words, "God be merciful to me a sinner and save me for Christ's sake," that then all of our life is over and we've lived the sinner's life we will ultimately be saved by grace!

The New Testament has a lot to say about the Christian life and the sin that is a part of that life, but one thing that a Christian is never called is a "sinner saved by grace." We are in fact Saints saved by grace!

Christians are called "saints" over 60 times in the New Testament! A saint is one who is sacred, pure, consecrated and most holy. On the other hand the unsaved are called "sinners" over 40 times in the New Testament. Such careless teaching that we are "sinners saved by grace" has produced a bad attitude toward the Christian experience. Christians are *saints* saved by grace. They are holy children, sacred to God and they are pure and consecrated to the purposes of God.

We often think of Sainthood in terms of Christians who were in some way especially holy like St. John or St. Paul, but everyone who has received Christ is a saint. Think of it, you are a Saint! Try putting the word, saint, in front of your name, Saint Alice, Saint Robert, Saint Richard! It not only sounds great, but it's theologically sound. We should address each other this way! Think what would happen in our church life if we would begin addressing each other as Saint_____! We would, no doubt, have greater respect for each other and for ourselves! "That sounds like boasting or self exaltation," you say. Well, then, we should remember the words of the Lord to Peter who said, "What God hath cleansed, that call not thou common," Acts 10:15.

It's a fact that we are a saint, generally, and no longer a sinner. Let's rejoice in sainthood!

The Specialties of Saints

Image bearers. Ephesians 2:10 reminds us that, "we are His workmanship created in Christ Jesus unto good works, which God hath before ordained that we should walk in them." Saints are preordained to good works and holy living. I Peter 1:13-16 asks us to "gird up the loins of your mind, be sober, and hope to the end for the grace that is to be brought to you at the revelation of Jesus Christ: as obedient children, not fashioning yourselves according to the former lusts in your ignorance: but as he which hath called you is holy so be ye holy in all manner of conversation; because it is written, Be ye holy, for I am holy." Peter is asking us to act like God and this would be an impossible task were it not for the presence of God within us to reveal Himself through us.

Saints are specially equipped to be "image bearers." Paul says in Galatians 1:15-16 that God called him by his grace to reveal His Son in him. As a Christian we possess the presence of God within us and by faith we have the privilege of enabling the God of glory to manifest himself not only to the unregenerate world about us but to His precious church for which He gave Himself.

As our life with Christ progresses we should become more adept at revealing Christ through us. The knowledge of the Word in spiritual understanding produces the revelation of God in our lives. cf. II Corinthians 3:18, James 1:22-25.

Some things that hinder the expression of Christ through our lives are a failure to allow the Word of God to work in the "image bearing" process as is illustrated by the Christian Saints who counteracted the life-changing affect of the word through carnality, I Corinthians 3:1-4. The Hebrew Christians also counteracted the affect of the life-changing affect of the Word through adhering to a religious traditionalism

that wouldn't allow them to fully accept the eternal priesthood of Christ. These things are still problems for us as
image bearers today, but if you'll read on I have some
solutions! Nevertheless, all of us are "image bearers" and
will ultimately achieve a degree of success because of a pre-
planned process. Romans 8:29 tells us, "He also did pre-
destinate us to be conformed to the image of His Son."
Praise the Lord! You're probably a better "image bearer"
than you think. After all, you are a saint, aren't you?

Fruit bearing. What do you mean by fruit bearing?
Galatians 5:22 says the fruit of the spirit is love, joy, peace,
longsuffering, gentleness, goodness, faith, meekness, tem-
perance. It is the desire of the Lord to produce these Christ-
like characteristics in us and they do become the hallmark
of Christian character to some degree in every Christian.

Fruit is also a necessity for continuation of a species.
Reproduction is a part of life, itself. Saints are especially
enabled to be fruitbearers. John 15:16 reminds us of the *cer-
tainty* of fruitbearing.

John 15:4 and 5 reminds us of the *process* of fruitbearing. Matthew 13:23 tells is of the *requirement* for fruitbearing.
John 12:24 reveals the *cost* of fruitbearing. Some saints are
concerned about their ability to produce fruit, and we all
should be because it's a part of sainthood. However, the last
thing I want to do is to put you on a guilt trip concerning how
many souls you have, personally introduced to Christ.
After all, it is God's work to introduce Himself to others
through us. In I Corinthians 3:6-9 Paul tells us that it is
"God that giveth the increase" and that we are "laborers
together" in the fruitbearing process.

Fruitbearing is not something we must strive for but
simply let happen. When the time and conditions are right
reproduction takes place naturally and joyfully. In fact, the
various "guilt trips" that we assume as Christians are probably the greatest deterrant to the outworking of Christ in

our lives.

I like what Pete Gillquist says in his book, *"Love is Now"*[1] concerning a young man who was reluctant to become a Christian because he would have to become a witness for Christ if he were saved. Peter assured him that he could become a Christian without doing a thing for Christ. The result was that he received Christ and immediately spread the news around the fraternity house about a salvation that could be received without doing anything! The attitude makes a difference! After all, you are a saint, aren't you?

[1]Peter Gillquist, *Love Is Now* (Grand Rapids, Michigan; Zondervan Publishing House, 1970), pp.94-95

Chapter 9

Traditional Ritual Baptismal Regeneration

I. Introduction.

Baptism, by the mode of immersion and sprinkling, has been performed as a means of producing or receiving salvation from the earliest times in the Christian faith. In Acts 8:13 to 23 Phillip, the evangelist, baptised Simon, the sorcerer, but even though Simon believed the word and was baptised, as others who believed, he remained unregenerate. Regeneration unto eternal life can only occur by the regenerating power of the Holy Spirit.

Article 28 of the Westminister Confession of Faith 1643 states, "All that are baptised are undoubtedly regenerated" after having said, "not only those that actually profess faith and obedience unto Christ, but also the infants of one or both believing parents are to be baptised."[1] Thus, through such confessions of faith and the inherent desire of denominations to institutionalize tradition, the doctrine

---

[1]Henry Bettenson, *Documents of the Christian Church* (Oxford University Press, 1943), p. 351

persists until now.

The word, baptism, in the Greek means to dip or immerse. It is used to describe both the ritual and spiritual baptism of believers as well as other concepts of baptism in the New Testament scriptures.

Ritual baptism refers to the rite of baptism in which a person is either immersed in water or sprinkled with water.

Spiritual baptism refers to the regenerating process of the Holy Spirit whereby a person, by faith in Jesus Christ, is regenerated to new life and is converted from his old nature to a new creation in Christ. He not only acquires a new personality as a result of his surrender to Jesus Christ but is "automatically" incorporated or "immersed" in the spiritual body of Christ called the Church.

Several New Testament illustrations are used to describe this spiritual baptism of believers. Ritual baptism is an illustration of spiritual baptism. cf. I Peter 3:21.

Planting is an illustration of spiritual baptism. cf. Romans 6:5. Just as a seed is planted and dies and decays to produce new life from the ground, so one who dies to self rises to new life in Christ. cf. John 12:24, 25

Crucifixion is an illustration of spiritual baptism. Like Jesus Christ who was crucified and died on the cross and was buried to rise again in resurrection on the third day, even so, anyone who "dies" in the surrender of his life and allows himself to be "spiritually" buried with Jesus Christ will rise to new life by the process of surrender.

Although the word, baptism, means to dip or immerse, the concept of a change of environment seems to be a part of the definition of the word in its New Testament uses. In the symbolic uses of the word to describe spiritual baptism, a body is changed from the environment of filth to cleanliness, a seed is changed from the environment of decay to new life and a body is taken from a dark grave and transferred to a bright environment of a new life.

There are many kinds of baptism in the New Testament that fall into the two general classications of ritual or spiritual baptism. I have been able to separate thirteen different kinds of baptism in the New Testament which has, no doubt, led to the traditional teaching of baptismal regeneration. When the word, baptise, is understood in its general sense rather than a narrow, specific sense of ritual baptism the traditional teaching of baptismal regeneration cannot be supported by scripture.

II. Here, then, are the thirteen kinds of baptism I have discovered in the New Testament.

A. The first kind of baptism described is John's baptism in Matthew 3:7. John's message which led the Jews to the water of *ritual* baptism in the Jordan River is found in Matthew 3:2, "Repent ye: for the kingdom of heaven is at hand." John, the forerunner of Jesus Christ was preparing the Jews for the coming of Jesus Christ. Hearts prepared by repentance and the outward evidence of repentance through ritual baptism were prepared to hear and follow the Lord Jesus Christ.

B. The second kind of baptism in the New Testament is a *spiritual* baptism of believers into the gifts of the Holy Spirit, Matthew 3:11. John prophecied of Jesus Christ that, "he shall baptise you with the Holy Ghost." This promise is repeated through the gospels and the first chapter of Acts where Jesus repeats the prophecy and says it will happen, "not many days hence," Acts 1:5. In Acts 1:8 Jesus tells his disciples that the gift will enable them to be witnesses, and in Acts 2:1-11 the actual bestowal of the gift of witnessing takes place. This baptism of the gift of witnessing to lost Jews was prophesied in Isaiah 28:11-12. cf., also, I Corinthians 14:21. Peter calls it a gift baptism in Acts 11:17.

C. A third kind of baptism found in this same verse (Matthew 3:11) is the spiritual baptism of "fire." "He shall baptise you with the Holy Ghost, and with fire." Some have wrongly assumed that the expression, "Holy Ghost and fire" is speaking of one baptism. They say that the fulfillment of this baptism is seen at Pentecost where the Holy Spirit descended in a mighty rushing wind and "cloven tongues of fire" "sat upon each of them." This interpretation seems logical if the 11th verse is taken with Acts 2:1-3. However, if the 12th verse of Matthew 3 is included with the 11th verse a completely different interpretation comes forth. The reminder of the apostle Peter is very important at this point as he declares, "no prophecy of scripture is of any private interpretation," II Peter 1:20. Scripture cannot be pulled out of context. To do so is to abort the true meaning. Acts 1:5 deletes "and fire." Is Jesus Christ careless at this point in leaving out these words? No, he is not, because they are not part of the prophecy that is shortly to unfold for the disciples. The fire spoken of in Matthew 3:11 is the fire of judgement. John the Baptist is preaching to those who will be believers and to some who will never become believers. The believers will be baptised with the Holy Spirit. The unbelievers will be baptised with the fire of judgement. Verse 12 says that Jesus Christ holds a fan in his hand to separate the believers from the unbelievers. "He will burn up the chaff with unquenchable fire."

    D. The fourth kind of baptism spoken of in the New Testament is a *ritual* baptism of Jesus Christ, Matthew 3:16. Jesus came to John the Baptist to be baptised by him. John was baptising unto repentance so he refused Jesus Christ and said that he needed to be baptised by Jesus. cf. verse 14. However, when Jesus said, "Suffer it to be so now: for thus it becometh us to fulfill all righteousness," John baptised him. Certainly, Jesus Christ, the sinless one, did not need to be baptised unto repentance. One of the purposes of his baptism was the witness of the Father and the Spirit in the approval of His ministry, Matthew 13:16, 17. It seems to me that Jesus was also establishing this rite as an identification of his place in the church he would spiritually form. In Matthew 28:19 he commands his disciples to make disciples by teaching and to confirm disciples by baptism. How natural, then, for the founder of the church, to identify himself with his church in a sign of confirmation, cf. Hebrews 2:10-18, I Peter 2:4-8.

E. The fifth kind of baptism spoken of in the New Testament is Jesus Christ's *spiritual* baptism into suffering. cf. Matthew 20:22-23. When Jesus asks his disciples if they are able "to drink of the cup" that he would drink of and "be baptised with the baptism he would be baptised with?" they answered they were. He then agreed with them that they would drink of his cup and share his baptism. It seems to me that the reference to the cup relates to Luke 22:42 where Jesus Christ seeks deliverance from the "cup." Some commentators have suggested that this refers to his fear and distaste for Calvary's cross upon which he soon would be nailed. I can't believe this because of his repeated predictions of the cross being his whole purpose for coming to earth. cf. Matthew 12:40, Mark 6:21, Mark 8:31, Mark 9:31, Luke 9:22, John 12:27-33. Also, the Old Testament prophesied his determination to fulfill this purpose, Isaiah 50:6, 7. It seems more logical to me that the attack of Satan upon himself and his disciples was the cup to which he referred. It was *this* cup that his disciples would share and not the cross.

In John 14:30 Jesus prophesied of the coming of satan. This visitation of satan occurred between the last supper and the cross. Since there is a limited amount of scripture for this period of time, Matthew 26:36-46 and Luke 22:39-46 describe the effort of satan to either divert or destroy Jesus Christ from completing his task in earth, the substitutionary death of the cross for the lost. cf. II Corinthians 5:21. The emotional agony of Jesus Christ and the strange drowsiness of the disciples, as well as their later conduct, attest to the visitation of Satan, a baptism of suffering in which they all shared. cf. Luke 22:53.

F. A sixth kind of baptism is the *ritual* baptism of Jesus' disciples, offered to the repentant. Jesus preached the same message as John the baptist, "repent: for the kingdom of heaven is at hand." cf. Matthew 4:17. Therefore, the same evidence or confirmation of repentance was requir-ed, a ritual baptism of repentance. Although Jesus, himself, never baptised the repentants his disciples did fulfill this ministry. cf. John 4:2.

G. A seventh kind of baptism presented in the New Testament is a *ritual* baptism unto the receiving of the Holy Spirit. Of all the kinds and descriptions of baptism in the New Testament this is the only case where believers are regenerated through the process of the rite of baptism. This is the only time it occurs and there is no indication of it ever happening again. Peter was preaching to the Jewish nation as a result of a Spirit Baptism unto the gift of witnessing. He concludes his message with these words, in Acts 2:38, "repent and be baptised everyone of you in the name of Jesus Christ for the remission of sins, and ye shall receive the gift of the Holy Ghost." Here, repentance and baptism are pre-requisite to the *receiving of the Holy Spirit.* Why is this, when after Acts 8:37 baptism always *follows* the receiving of the Holy Spirit? This is a transitional method of regeneration for the Jew which never occurs again. In Acts 8:17 it is the laying on of hands which causes the disciples to *receive the Holy Spirit.* The *baptism* which had worked for the Jews in Acts 2:38-41 didn't work at all for the Samari-tans. It wasn't until Peter and John laid their hands upon them that they *received* the Holy Spirit.

This transitional experience of salvation for Jews, Samaritans, and Gentiles is related to Jesus Christ's pro-phecy of the use of the *Keys* given to apostle Peter, and will explain why different modes of salvation were occuring at this time in the history of the Church.

1. The Keys of the Kingdom of Heaven
Matthew 16:19

a. Introduction

In this study the meaning of the keys to the kingdom of heaven will be explained from reference of Scripture.

(1) In the complete context of scripture for the word "key," there are only eight references. These references are: Judges 3:25, Isaiah 22:22, Luke 11:52, Revelation 1:18, Revelation 3:7, 9:1, 20:1 and Matthew 16:19. The generally observed meaning of "key" is that which is familiar to the English; an opener or a key to a lock. We must conclude that Jesus Christ is promising to give Peter, himself, an opener or key to the lock for the kingdom of heaven.

(2) Secondly, concerning the context of this passage of Scripture, there are only two uses of the word key in the plural. These passages are: Matthew 16:19 and Revelation 1:18. Peter is given the "keys" to the kingdom of heaven and Christ holds the "keys" of hell and death. There is no apparent relationship between these two plural uses of the word, so we must examine the context of Matthew 16:19 for further clues to its meaning.

(3) We note from the immediate context of Matthew 16:19 that there are three subjects considered in this passage concerning the keys to be given to Peter.

(a) The subject of the ability for Peter to identify Jesus Christ as "the Christ, the Son of the living God," through the spiritual influence of the Father in heaven, in contrast to so many others who could not identify Him as the Christ. Matthew 16:13-14.

(b) The subject of the future church that Christ would build of men like Peter. Compare Peter's relationship to the foundation of the "spiritual house" that Christ will build. (Ephesians 2:20-22, Christ the cornerstone; the apostles the foundation stones; the believers the building stones, I Peter 2:5-6, I Corinthians 3:11.)

(c) The subject of binding and loosing is also a part of the context of this passage of scripture. The ability of Peter to bind on earth becomes effective in heaven and his ability to loose on earth is also effective in heaven.

We may summarize the immediate context this way. Jesus Christ is at the time he is speaking to Peter, promising to build a spiritual house of believers of whom Peter is a part. Peter and all others who become a part of this church will testify that "Jesus is the Christ," the Son of the living God by the spiritual insight given them by the Father.

Peter in some way holds the key to this revelation of Christ and his church, and has the power to both bind and loose as a part of this function.

b. In the first area of investigation of this scripture, we will need a more complete definition of "binding and loosing." There are only two passages in Scripture that speak of binding and loosing. They are Matthew 16:19 and Matthew 18:15-20, but there is one other scripture which must be included with these two because of the similarity of word meanings and the obvious parallelism of "remitting and retaining," the context of the church, and the context of the ministry of the disciples, and the prophesy of the "keys." This scripture is John 20:23, and it, once again, is a very limited concept, occurring only once in scripture.

(1) In Matthew 16:19, binding and loosing is used with reference to the building of the church. cf. Matthew 16:18. In other words Peter is the key or has the keys necessary for initiating the building of the church. It is awesome to contemplate that God directs His omnipotence through the weakness of human flesh. Our Savior accomplished the redemption of creation in the weakness of human flesh and it was prophesied of Saul of Tarsus, a former enemy of the church, that he would build the church by bearing the name of Christ before the Gentiles, kings and the children of Israel; Acts 9:15. So successfully did he complete the task that he testified to Timothy, "I have fought a good fight, I have finished my course," II Timothy 4:7. Peter could testify the same, for he faithfully opened the doors of salvation to the lost through the ministry of the Holy Spirit through his life. It is well to remember, at this point, that the excluded member does not lose his salvation.

(2) In Matthew 18:15-20, "binding and loosing" is not a ministry to *initiate* the building of the church, but is a part of this ministry of *maintainance* of the future church. It is found in the context of responsible church fellowship towards the "little ones" (Matthew 18:10) in the church; those that have gone astray from the church (Matthew 18:12) and those that offend the church (Matthew 18:12). The future churches will be granted the power to discipline their fellowships.

They will follow the procedure prescribed by the Lord in verses 15-17 and if one who is called a brother fails to respond to exhortation, he will be loosed from local church fellowship, verse 18.

This action is not only expressed on earth but registered also in heaven. cf. I Corinthians 5:11, Romans 16:17, II Thessalonians 3:14. Verses 19 and 20 remind us that a church fellowship exercises a resposibility to its membership and that Christ, himself, governs in the midst of his churches. (Revelation 1:20.)

So decisive is the action of a church in the separation of an unrepentant member that Paul can say in I Corinthians 5:5 that "they may be delivered to satan for the destruction of the flesh" and I Corinthians 5:13 "them that are without, God judgeth." The destruction is not to his spiritual life, but of his flesh. cf. I Corinthians 3:15. It is also good to remember that the separation of the member is for the benefit of both the church (I Corinthians 5:6-7) and the member, that he might be reclaimed for Christ. (II Corinthians 2:6-11.)

In the Matthew 16 account of "binding and loosing," the salvation of unsaved souls to be included in the church is in view. In the Matthew 18 account of "binding and loosing," the well-being of the local church is in view.

(3)   In John 20:23, many similarities of context point to the fact that this scripture should reveal light on Matthew 16:19. In both passages, Jesus is alone with his disciples; the subject of the church is in view, an awesome responsibility is placed on Peter in Matthew 16:19 and then upon all the disciples in John 20:23 and the prophecy of the "keys" and their use is still before Peter. It appears in John 20:23 that the other disciples are in some way to share in Peter's use of the "keys."

c. A second area of investigation that relates to an understanding of the keys given to Peter and the awesome
power that they give him, is the beginning of the church
and its manifestation in the first local assembly of
believers who qualify in every way as a local church. It
seems to me from the account in John 20:19-23, that the
first local church came into existance and the first
nucleus church was made up of the risen Lord and his
disciples in the upper room. Many have suggested that
the church began at Pentecost, but it is my conviction
that that which occurred at Pentecost, was Peter's first
experience with the keys of the kingdom of heaven. To
verify the actual beginning of the first local church let us
list the characteristics of a local church.

(1) They are by their very name "called out ones,"
("the doors were shut where the disciples were
assembled," John 20:19.)

(2) They are under the Lordship of Christ; Ephesians
1:22-23, 4:15, 5:23 ("Came Jesus and stood in the
midst," John 20:19) ("so send I you," John 20:21.)

(3) They are redeemed by Christ; Ephesians 5:25,
("He showed them His hands and His side,"
John 20:20.)

(4) They are indwelt by God's spirit; John 14:17,
Romans 8:9-11, I Corinthians 3:16, I Corinthians
6:19. ("receive ye the Holy Ghost," John 20:22.)

(5) They are also baptised into the body of Christ.
John 17:18-23; (verse 21 – "that they also may be
one in us"); (verse 18 – "sent"); (verse 23 – *"perfect* in one") NOTE: John 14:20, indwelling and
baptizing are seen as a simultaneous act of God.
To be indwelt by God's spirit, is to be baptized by
God's spirit into Christ. This complete unity happens at Spiritual rebirth. John 20:21, "as the Father

hath sent me," (in unity with Himself) even so send I you (in unity with me). There is no scripture that teaches that spiritual baptism into the body of Christ occurs *after* spirit indwelling!

(6) They are fed by an undershepherd; Ephesians 4:11, Acts 20:28, I Peter 5:1-2, (John 21:16, "feed my sheep)."

Certainly the Lord and his disciples meet these six tests of a local church, and since they do, there must be a difference between the prophesied gift baptism of the spirit in the gospels and the spirit baptism of I Corinthians 12:13, into the body of Christ.

d. Therefore, a third area of investigation that relates to an understanding of the keys of the kingdom of heaven given to Peter is that of *baptism*. The word itself means, to immerse or to dip; to dye; resulting in a word of dipping, immersing; cleansing by washing, and the rite of baptism.

It is my conviction that the baptism which occurred at Pentecost was a baptism of spiritual gifts, and that this was prophesied by John the Baptist of Jesus Christ in Matthew 3:11 and by Christ in John 7:38-39, Acts 1:5 and Acts 1:8. This baptism is described as an "upon" ministry in Acts 1:8 and Acts 2:3 and produced gifted, Spirit-empowered preaching through the lives of those who had already "received" the spirit; John 20:22. It is interesting to note the sequence of events that preceed this baptism of spiritual gifts from John 7:38-39.

Following in the reverse order of presentation from the last part of verse 39 we discover, (1) Jesus must be glorified, (He is a risen conquering Lord) (2) The receiving of the Holy Spirit, (indwelling presence) (3) The flowing of rivers of living water out of his belly, (the experience at Pentecost). The order thus follows: Christ is raised, the Holy Spirit is received, and the Holy Spirit flows from lives.

e. It is my conviction that Peter was the key man in three separate uses of the "keys of the kingdom" in opening salvation to all men. At Jerusalem Peter became the spokesman for the disciples after the display of the baptism of gifts and instructed the *Jewish* populace to "repent and be baptized in the name of Jesus Christ for the remission of sins" and they would *"receive the gift* of the Holy Ghost."

Peter's first key unlocked the doors of salvation to the Jews at Jerusalem and all over the world. Perhaps this is what Paul has in mind in Romans 1:16 when he says, "to the Jew first."

About a year later when the persecution of Jewish Christians at Jerusalem became intense, some of them dispersed to outlying areas. Phillip went down to Samaria (Acts 8:5) and preached Christ to them, but, even though they believed Phillip (Acts 8:12) and were baptized (Acts 8:12) the Holy Spirit had not come to them. Samaritans were half breed Jews so couldn't receive the provision of the key of salvation which Peter provided for the Jews. It remained for Peter and John to lay hands on the Samaritan and *then* they *received* the Holy Ghost. (Acts 8:17.)

About eight years later Peter is constrained by a vision from heaven to meet Cornelius, a Gentile. (Acts 10:21-22.) But even though Cornelius "feared God," (Acts 10:22), and "prays" and "gives" to God, (Acts 10:4), he still has not received the Holy Spirit. It remains for Peter to explain the way of salvation, (Acts 10:43), and while he is doing this a gift baptism of speaking in tongues is witnessed by the Jewish evangelists which to them is a certain evidence that they have *received* the

Holy Spirit. (Acts 10:47, cf. also I Corinthians 14:21-22.) So Peter was there for the third time, the key man with the "keys" of the kingdom of heaven to open the doors of salvation to all the lost. This faithfully fulfills Christ's prophecy of Peter's ministry and Christ's prophecy of the order of that ministry in Acts 1:8, "in Jerusalem and Judea," the key to the Jews; "and in Samaria," the key to the Samaritans; "and unto the uttermost part of the earth," the key to the Gentiles salvation. Please note also from Acts 1:1 that Jesus is addressing his Acts 1:8 prophecy "unto the apostles whom he had chosen," which is the antecedant of the *"ye"* of Acts 1:8.

f. It now becomes necessary to explain the seemingly contradictory order of events in the use of the keys by Peter.

   (1) First of all, it is an established fact in the context of New Testament history of the churches that the order of events in the salvation of the lost is the witness by three basic ingredients for the establishment of faith in the unsaved, (the Word, the Spirit, the man) (I Thessalonians 1:5) produce faith (Romans 10:17) which produces the fruit of salvation, namely, repentance, baptism, good works. Ephesians 2:8-10. God saves us, Romans 3:21-25, and not works. (Acts 16:31, Romans 10:9-10, Galatians 3:2-5.)

   (2) In Peter's use of the keys to the Jews at Jerusalem, an interesting order of events takes place which produced for those *first* converts a Spirit indwelt salvation. In Acts 2:38, Peter commands, repent, be baptized in the name of Jesus for the remission of sins, and ye shall receive the gift of the Holy Ghost. We may assume that in a true spirit of

repentance, *as* the disciples baptized them in the name of Jesus, the Holy Spirit was *received* and they were born again. This would seem to be a contradiction to Ephesians 2:8-9 which says we are saved by grace through faith without works under which both repentance and baptism must be included. There are three things that must be noted in commentary on this unusual method of Spiritual rebirth.

(a) This is the *only* place in the New Testament where salvation is received through baptismal repentance.

(b) The Jewish people, following this event, never received spiritual rebirth by this means again. Acts 4:4, 5:14. In Acts 9, the order of spiritual rebirth for Saul of Tarsus (a Hebrew of Hebrews) is clearly set forth. First he had faith in the Lord (Acts 9:6) then, he was healed and *finally,* he was baptized. The same order of spiritual rebirth is given for the Jewish proselyte of Ethiopia (Acts 8:27, who *first* believes, (Acts 8:34-37) with all his heart and then, is baptized as a testimony of his faith.

(c) Peter's Pentecostal message is addressed specifically to the Jewish race, the *"house of Israel,"* (Acts 2:36, Acts 5:31), and not to unsaved Jews, as such, thus linking this unique transitional message to the keys offered to Peter by our Lord Jesus Christ and to the message preached by John the Baptist to Israel. (Matthew 3:2, "Repent ye for the *kingdom* of heaven is at hand.") and the message of our Lord to Israel, (Matthew 4:17), "Repent for the *kingdom* of heaven is at hand.") Peter's Pentecostal message is unique in many ways, in that, it was preached to the *nation of Jews* with adequate representation. (Acts 2:9-11.) It was transitional and in context with the message of John the Baptist and Christ, it was the fulfillment in part of Joel's prophecy (cf. Joel 2:28-29) to the Jews, and finally, met the fulfillment of Christ's prophecy to Peter that he would unlock the door of salvation to the Jewish people. For those Jews who believed Peter and were baptized and born again, *the kingdom had come* and was no longer "at hand." (Matthew 11:12-15, Malachi 4:5-6.)

(3) In Peter's use of the key's to the Samaritans, the opposite order of events take place. When at Jerusalem, baptism and repentance were prerequisite to spiritual rebirth, while now at the use of Peter's second key these things are shown to be totally irrelevant to spiritual rebirth for in the case of Simon who both believes Phillip and is baptized, (Acts 8:13) we see one who is not spiritually reborn and over whom there is a serious doubt that he ever will be spiritually reborn. (Acts 8:20-25.)

The order of events for the Samaritan's salvation seem to be:

(a) An *initial* introduction to the process of Spiritual rebirth through the preaching of the word by a servant of the Lord. Acts 8:5-8.

(b) The culmination of faith in the testimony of baptism. (Acts 8:12.) However, Peter is the key to their spiritual rebirth *as a race.* The words of the Lord to Peter are once again impressed upon him as he said, "whatsoever thou shalt bind on earth shall be bound in heaven:

and whatsoever thou shalt loose on earth shall be loosed in heaven."

(c) Peter is called to Samaria and in the simple process of *laying his hands on these believers* they *receive* the Holy Ghost. (Acts 8:17.) This also is a unique experience of spiritual rebirth and the laying on of hands is never again a part of the process of spiritual rebirth. There is no indication that Peter, himself, ever followed this practice again. (Acts 8:25.)

(d) It is noteworthy that there is no manifestation of a "gift baptism" here at Samaria, and we may rightly conclude that it was not part of the prophetic future for the Samaritans as it was for the Jews, a "sign-seeking race" (Matthew 12:39, I Corinthians 14:21, Isaiah 28:11-12, Joel 2:28, Acts 2:16).

(4) In Peter's final use of the keys with reference to the church which was to include both Jew and Gentile alike (Ephesians 3:6, Ephesians 2:14) and even the Samaritans which were neither Jew nor Gentile, (John 4:9) we see the doors of salvation open to a people in a manner closest of all three to the New Testament pattern of spiritual rebirth.

(a) The manner of spiritual rebirth is presented to the Gentiles (Acts 10:43). Peter says to "believe" in Christ is to "receive" remission of sins.

(b) While Peter is preaching, the Holy Spirit ministers spiritual rebirth through faith (Acts 10:44). As a result of receiving the spirit *within*, a "gift baptism" of the spirit produces an *outpouring* of evidence. (John 7:38-39.) The spirit cannot flow *out* until He has come *within*.

(c) It is noteworthy at this point to mention that, like the Samaritans, the Gentiles also had no prophetic future with reference to tongues and, yet, at the opening of the door of their salvation they express this "gift baptism" of tongues. The answer to this expression of a "gift baptism" becomes quite apparent when we examine the context. It is not for the Gentiles benefit that they speak with tongues, but for the Jewish evangelists that are present, so that they will understand that the Gentiles also are included in spiritual rebirth and in the church. Peter knew that they could not have the "gift baptism" without first having received the spirit. (Acts 10:47.) their ritual baptism also follows their spiritual rebirth. (verse 48.)

(d) It is also noteworthy that the "gift baptism" was the same kind of a manifestation that had occurred at Pentecost of Acts 11:14-18, in that the tongues spoken were understood by the hearers as a known language. (Acts 2:6-11.)

(e) It is also interesting to note that there follows after this final use of the keys by Peter an "open" preaching of the gospel and a universal spiritual rebirth for all who believe. (Acts 11: 19-21, Acts 13:1-4, Acts 13:49, Acts 15:13-18, Galatians 2:7-8.)

Although Acts 2:38, which is a ritual baptism unto the receiving of the Holy Spirit, has taken a lengthy explanation of the transitional period from the Old Testament to the New Testament it is a key passage in understanding the error of traditional baptism regeneration. If this passage is isolated from the rest of New Testament scripture this text provides proof that baptism is necessary for regeneration, i.e. the receiving of the Holy Spirit. It is a key text for those who teach regeneration by baptism. We can certainly be thankful that the scripture certifies that interpretation relies on the Holy Spirit and context (cf. I Corinthians 2:10-13, II Peter 1:19-21) or we would be in a state of confusion concerning this doctrine.

H. The eighth kind of baptism in the New Testament is Phillip's *ritual* baptism in Acts 8:12. This baptism seems to serve no purpose at all. It does not produce a receiving of the Holy Spirit as it did in Acts 2:38. Neither is it a sign or evidence of regenerate faith as it later becomes in the New Testament, for the Holy Spirit is received by the laying on of hands, verse 17, *after* ritual baptism. This experience of salvation for the Samaritans teaches us that baptism is not a part of the receiving of the Holy Spirit and that the laying on of hands by Peter is necessary for the receiving of the Holy Spirit. As has already been explained, Peter is making a second use of the "keys of the kingdom." Later, in the New Testament after the opening of the door of salvation to the Samaritan race and the Gentile race, Peter is no longer a necessary part of the receiving of the Holy Spirit, and neither is the laying on of hands. A possible reason for the baptism of Phillip is to reveal to Phillip and the Samaritans that baptism is not essential to regeneration. Phillip's experience at Jerusalem had been that baptism produced regeneration as he watched what happened on the day of Pentecost. He, no doubt, preached this doctrine to the Samaritans not realizing that the message Peter preached at Jerusalem to the Jews was a special message for them as a race. Thus, the doctrine of salvation by grace without works is being reinforced by the ministry of the Holy Spirit. When Simon seeks to buy the power from Peter, Acts 8:18-24, Peter rebukes him for suggesting that regeneration can be purchased or earned in any way. Salvation is received by *grace alone,* through faith.

I. The ninth kind of baptism in the New Testament is believer's *ritual* baptism as experienced by the Ethiopian eunuch in Acts 8:38. Although the Ethiopian was a Jewish pilgrim, his regeneration occurred through the *spiritual understanding* of the scriptures. cf. Acts 8:28-35. It is apparent from this scripture that baptism is a public testimony of the spiritual regeneration that occurs by hearing and believing the scriptures which reveal Jesus Christ as God's propitious sacrifice for our sin and our Lord, verses 32-37. The command for disciples' baptism was both taught by Phillip and understood by the Ethiopian (cf. Matthew 28:19, Acts 8:38). Even though Peter's final use of the "keys" is yet to be experienced by the Gentile race, the pattern of testimonial ritual baptism is being established for Jewish converts.

J. The tenth kind of baptism in the New Testament is *spiritual* baptism into regeneration. Romans 6:4. This spiritual baptism occurs as a result of the spirit of God making the preaching of the Word so clear to an individual that he believes Jesus Christ died on the cross for his personal sin and that the blood of Jesus has washed all of the sins away. He also recognizes that Jesus Christ has risen from the grave as almighty God in human flesh and that He is the Lord of his life. cf. Romans 10:9-10. This spiritual surrender of his life to Jesus Christ results in the crucifixion of his old personality and the resurrection of a new personality within his human flesh. (cf. II Corinthians 5:17, Galatians 2:20.) This *spiritual baptism* into death produces regenerate life in Jesus Christ.

K. The eleventh kind of baptism described in the New Testament is the *spiritual* baptism of Moses' leadership, I Corinthians 10:2. This means that as Israel was led out of Egypt under the leadership of Moses they all experienced the accompanying manifestation of the miracles of God. They were baptised into an environment of the experiences of God's miraculous power. They all saw the cloud of God over them in the daytime. They saw the pillar of fire during the night. They all went through the Red Sea on dry land because of the miracle of God. They all drank the miraculously supplied water of God in the dessert. Israel was baptised into the miraculous presence of God under the leadership of Moses.

L. The twelfth kind of baptism is the *ritual* baptism for the dead in I Corinthians 15:29. Many strange doctrines have arisen from this verse such as proxy ritual baptism for unsaved dead in order to confer eternal life upon them. Such interpretations that discredit a personal faith in Jesus Christ and salvation by grace through faith cannot be considered to have any truth. Also, the opportunity for a second chance for salvation after this life is not taught in scripture.

Within the context of baptism in the New Testament scriptures there is only one interpretation that also fits the context of this passage. The apostle has the resurrection in mind as he makes this statement. He also has in mind the suffering that we go through in these mortal bodies as we sacrifice our lives for Christ.

In verse 26 he says the last enemy to be abolished is "death." The last part of a Christian to be restored to life is the body. The spirit is made alive, a new creation by faith in Jesus Christ, but the body is unaffected by spiritual regeneration. In Romans 8:11-12 Paul reasons that because Christ's spirit will one day resurrect these mortal bodies to immortality we are indebted to the Spirit to live for Christ by the mortification of the deeds of the body. In other words, it makes sense to live a sacrificial life for Christ in view of the resurrection of the body. Romans 8:23 says, "we groan within ourselves" waiting for the "redemption of our body."

Resurrection is a cardinal doctrine of Christian faith. When one is baptised as a witness for his faith in Christ, a part of that faith in Christ is the promised resurrection of the body. In Romans 7:24-25 Paul asks, "who shall deliver me from the body of this death?" Then he concludes by saying, "I thank God through Jesus Christ, our Lord."

In I Corinthians 15:31 Paul says, "I die daily," meaning that he has sacrificed his life to Christ on a daily basis. But if there is no hope of receiving a new body in resurrection for this dead body we must live in now, what is the point of having faith in Christ? When we were baptised as a testimony of our faith in Christ it was with the guarantee that our faith would produce a resurrected experience with Christ. "What will all of those Christians do who were baptised for those dead bodies if dead persons are not actually raised? Why, indeed, are they baptised on behalf of those dead bodies? (I Corinthians 15:29, my paraphrase.)

Paul continues this line of reasoning in verse 32 as he says, "If after the manner of men I have fought with beasts at Ephesus, what advantageth it me, if the dead rise not? Let us eat and drink: for tomorrow we die." This passage of scripture, then, deals with one aspect of Christian faith that is a part of the testimony of believer's ritual baptism.

M. The thirteenth kind of baptism in the New Testament is believers spiritual baptism into the body of Christ, the Church. At the time of spiritual regeneration into new life in Christ, the union of the believer to Jesus Christ also produces a union with all other believers. Ephesians 4:5. In I Corinthians 12:13 the scripture declares, "For by one spirit we are all baptised into the body, whether we be *Jews* or *Gentiles,* whether we be bond or free; and have been all made to drink into one spirit." The regeneration that produced the new life in Christ also produces a new relationship with the others who have been regenerated. The evidence of this new life and its new relationships is emphasized in the epistle of I John.

III. The scriptures used to support ritual baptismal regeneration.

Acts 2:38. To me, there is no question that baptism was prerequisite to the receiving of the Holy Spirit in this passage. The scripture cannot be used to support the doctrine in our time, however, because of its transitional Old Testament, New Testament purpose, it only occurs once in scripture, compared to many instances of believer's testimonial ritual baptism following this passage and salvation is received by grace through faith in Christ, alone, throughout the New Testament.

Mark 16:16. Although Mark 16:16 says, "He that believeth and is baptised shall be saved:" it does not say, "but he that believeth not *and is not baptised* shall be damned." Believing is necessary for salvation and baptism normally follows such faith but one is lost only through *not believing.*

I Peter 3:21. I Peter 3:21 says, "The like figure whereunto even baptism doth also now save us." This part of the verse when separated from the rest of the verse seems to teach ritual baptismal regeneration, however, the intent of Peter is not to teach regeneration through baptism but that a "good conscience" toward God is what saves us. He makes it quite clear that it is not the water of ritual baptism washing a filthy body but the spiritual exercise of a faithful testimony of suffering for Christ as He died for us. cf. I Peter 4:1, Acts 22:16, I Peter 3:16, "Having a good conscience."

Titus 3:5. "Not by works of righteousness which we have done, but according to his mercy he saved us, *by the washing of regeneration* and renewing of the Holy Ghost." This verse provides its own refutation for regeneration by ritual baptism. "Not by works of righteousness" would exclude baptism as a work of righteousness. Anything one would or could do, personally, for salvation must be classed as a work of righteousness. The washing of regeneration in this verse, no doubt, refers to the action of the word of God made clear by the Spirit of God to our hearts and minds. Such verse as Ephesians 5:26 makes it clear that God's word is able to wash our minds thus providing, through His mercy, the ability to believe and be saved by faith, alone. cf. I Corinthians 6:11, John 17:17, John 15:3. Salvation is made possible by God's Word. cf. James 1:18, I Peter 1:23.

John 3:5. "Jesus answered, "verily, verily, I say unto thee, except a man be born of water and of the spirit, he cannot enter into the kingdom of God." Three possible interpretations for the word "water" have come forth as interpretations for this verse. The water may mean the water of natural birth, for Nicodemus talks about the womb in verse 4 and Jesus answers in verse 6, "That which is born of flesh is flesh." This interpretation depends on what Jesus knew Nicodemus was thinking about when he asked the question.

Nicodemus was a teacher of Israel according the verse 10. We must conclude that he had a well established plan of salvation, according to the law, for Israelites that he taught and who believed. If Jesus was referring to the water of birth he would probably have answered, "Except a man be born of *Abraham* and of the spirit, he cannot enter the Kingdom of God." Both Gentiles and Jews are born into the world in the water of birth so if *only* birth had been necessary for entrance into the kingdom before Jesus adds the second "spirit birth" Gentiles and Jews would have had equal access to salvation. Nicodemus would never accept this theology.

Another possible interpretation for water is the "water of the word." As has been previously mentioned, Ephesians 5:26 speaks of the washing of water by the Word. Although this definition agrees with the overall context of the scripture it is difficult to fit into the narrow context of this passage of scripture. The Word of God and its sanctifying power has not been brought up in this conversation between Christ and Nicodemus. Here, we have a teacher of Jews who is convinced that Jesus is a teacher from God. He is confronted with a new theology of spiritual rebirth and is told that his theology is incomplete for entrance into the kingdom of God. Jesus, by his own confession has "not come to destroy, but to fulfill" the law. Matthew 5:17. Therefore, it seems to me that the word "water must mean the water of Jewish purification with which Nicodemus was very familiar. John 2:6 speaks of six waterpots containing approximately 20 gallons each that were used for Jewish purification ceremonies. cf. Exodus 30:18, II Chronicles 4:2, 6, Mark 7:3, 4. With the background of Jewish purification and with John the Baptist's ministry of baptising in the Jordan River unto repentance, cf. John 1:28, Jesus could not discredit water as a part of the preparation for entrance into the Kingdom of God. Nicodemus needed to know that such water cleansings as he performed and as John the Baptist performed were not sufficient in themselves for entrance into the Kingdom of God. The apostle Peter would tie both water and spirit rebirth together at Pentecost as he used the "keys of the kingdom" for the first time. cf. Acts 2:38. Then after the fulfillment of the use of this key, ritual washing would be replaced by the spiritual washing of God's word in producing spiritual rebirth.

IV. The scriptures that refute ritual baptismal regeneration.

To me, one of the strongest arguments against the tradition of ritual baptismal regeneration is the confession of Paul the apostle that he was not sent to baptise! cf. I Corinthians 1:17. Here is an apostle who was under the teaching of Jesus Christ on a one-to-one basis. cf. Galatians 1:11-18. he surely knew what was required for salvation. When he saw the divisions in the Corinthian Church he is thankful that he has not contributed to them by baptising. If baptism was necessary for salvation, surely Paul would want to baptise everyone he could irregardless of the division it might cause. The salvation of souls is more important than church division. Then, he specifically says, "Christ sent me not to baptise, but to preach the gospel." He thus excludes baptism from the gospel. It is not relevant to salvation.

The many scriptures that teach how one may be saved do not include baptism as a part of the teaching. cf. Romans 10:9-10, Romans 10:13, Acts 16:31, Ephesians 2:8-9, Romans 3:21-26, Romans 4:1-5.

The sequence of events that leads to baptism after the use of the "keys" given to Peter is always: 1. a hearing of the word, 2. believing the word through the illumination and regeneration of the Holy Spirit and 3. baptism as an outward confirmation of an inward conversion. Baptism is not a part of conversion but a witness of it.

V. The Purpose of Ritual Baptism.

1. Ritual baptism is an act of obedience to Christ.

In Matthew 28:19 Jesus commanded, "Go ye therefore, and teach all nations, baptising them in the name of the Father, and of the Son, and of the Holy Ghost." The disciples are to be obedient to the Lord's command to baptise the discipled. The discipled are to be obedient to the Lord by being baptised.

2. Ritual baptism is a mark of distinction for a believer.

When John the Baptist baptised Jesus he was distinctly approved by the Father and the Spirit, and established his oneness with those who would belong to him in the church. God specializes in tokens such as the rainbow, Genesis 9:12-13 and circumcision, Genesis 17:11, etc. No doubt the tokens of baptism and the Lord's supper are those that belong to the church.

3. Ritual baptism is a witness for the believer.

The Ethiopian requested baptism of Phillip in Acts 8:37. He, no doubt, wanted to testify to Phillip and to the caravan in which he was traveling that he was separating himself from Judaism to Christianity. For today's believer it is a witness of his separation from the world unto Christ. It is also a witness of the way he obtained salvation by the burial of himself with Christ and that he has arisen to new life in Christ. cf. Romans 6:3-10.

4. Ritual baptism is an expression of faith.

Since the Lord Jesus commanded baptism it is unthinkable that any who have received him as *Lord* would seek to disobey Him. Jesus asked the question himself. Luke 6:46, "And why call ye me, Lord, Lord, and do not the things which I say?" For many Christians it is the first outstanding expression of faith. The apostle Peter calls this expression of faith, "The answer of a good conscience toward God." cf. I Peter 3:21. Just as Noah's faith caused him to build an ark and enter it to escape from the judgement of the flood, so the Christian's faith causes him to be obedient to his Lord in the waters of baptism so that his faith is counted for righteousness. Real faith produces good works and among the first works is baptism. Ephesians 2:10, James 2:20.

VI. The Mode of Ritual Baptism.

One of the areas of tradition incorporated in traditional ritual baptismal regeneration is the practice of sprinkling the recipient with water or other things such as rose petals and pronouncing them "baptised."

The truth of the scripture teaches that *immersion* is the only acceptable mode of baptism.

1. *The definition of the word itself excludes sprinkling as a mode of baptism.* A lexical definition of the greek word, "bapto" is to dip, to dye, to immese, to cleanse or purify by washing. Sprinkling would fit none of these definitions.

2. *In the scripture, where the rite of baptism is performed much water is necessary.* cf. Acts 8:36-38, Mark 1:9, Matthew 3:6. Sprinkling would not require standing in a river. A cup of water is sufficient for sprinkling.

3. *The symbolic meaning of baptism as described in Romans 6:3-10 of the spiritual baptism into Christ can only be illustrated by immersion.* Christ's dead body rising from the grave cannot be illustrated by sprinkling. cf. Romans 6:4. Our dying to self which is illustrated by planting and rising to new life cannot be illustrated by sprinkling. cf. Romans 6:5.

If you have received Jesus Christ as your Savior and *Lord* the truth of scripture requires your obedience to the Lord in baptism by immersion as a testimony of your faith in Jesus Christ.

Conclusion

A. The scope of the book.

Truth vs. Tradition has examined some of the more important traditional concepts that are a hindrance to Christian faith. As well, there are some novelty traditional concepts that were included such as the "Christmas Tradition" and "We're Saints, Not Sinners" to show the extent to which we have traditionalized some of the doctrine of the Bible.

Basic faith in the finished work of Jesus Christ as sacrifice and priest, Savior and Lord, has not been annulled by tradition. As I stated in the introduction, "souls are still being saved, but there's a lot of faith being tarnished and a lot of joy being lost because of the overpowering influence of tradition."

It is my hope that the reader will begin to examine the Scriptures more carefully and compare what he reads with what he has been taught in his church, denomination, or seminary. It is also my hope that through the use of simple Bible study tools, others will join me in the search for Truth vs. Tradition.

"It was needful for me to write unto you, and exhort you that ye should earnestly contend for the faith which was once delivered unto the saints." Jude 3b.

These were more noble than those in Thessalonica, in that "they received the Word with all readiness of mind, and searched the Scriptures daily, whether those things were so." Acts 17:11.

B. The emphasis upon context.

As you have discovered, in reading "Truth vs. Tradition," a strong emphasis has been made on context for interpretation. I mentioned several reasons for the importance of context in interpretation in the introduction under the heading, "C. A Word about Hermaneutics."

It is axiomatic that since the author of the Bible is God and that God is perfect in mind and reason, that He has communicated a logical, congruous revelation of Himself to mankind. If there is contradictory doctrine, it has not come from God but from the influence of man on the Bible. The faithful student of the Word will seek to discover "original truth" on the principle of the congruity of the Bible according to the mind of God.

C. The style of writing.

You have, no doubt, had to stop and meditate and check the scriptural references to a given subject as you have been reading the book. You perhaps have wished that further explanations and illustrations had been given for the content.

If I had followed this style of writing the book would

have been much larger and more expensive.

Secondly, I would have been doing what I have been trying to discredit; i.e. the use of commentary to explain the Word of God rather than the use of the Word of God to explain itself.

"Howbeit when He, the Spirit of truth, is come, he will guide you into all truth" John 16:13a. "But the annointing which ye have received of Him abideth in you, and ye need not that any man teach you: but as the same annointing teacheth you of all things, and is truth, and is no lie, and even as it hath taught you, ye shall abide in him." I John 2:27.

D. The tools of contextual study.

As you have read the book you have perhaps been disappointed that I have used the King James version of the Bible rather than a modern language translation.

My reason for using the King James is because it is, first of all, a quite literal translation of the Scriptures. Many of the modern language translations contain paraphrase translation which allow for a greater influence of traditional teaching. Also, many authors of modern language translation appear to "follow the leader" in their translation interpretation.

Another reason for using the King James is that it is one of the few translations that has an exhaustive concordance produced for its text. An exhaustive concordance is a necessity for good contextual study of the Bible.

To those familiar with Biblical languages other concordances are also very helpful in contextual interpretation of Scripture.

Interlinear translations are also very helpful in contextual interpretation and can be used by those untrained in Bible languages.

E. A quote from James.

"My brethren, be not many masters (or teachers) knowing that we shall receive the greater condemnation (or judgement)." James 3:1.

James is saying we will be judged for what we teach! If we teach truth we receive reward, if we teach tradition contrary to truth we receive judgement. Teachers receive a greater judgement than others because the affect of their words is so great an influence upon the faith of others.

Therefore, we should be careful that the things we teach are really the Word and not extra-Biblical material that may be contrary to the Bible.

We should also exercise caution in accepting doctrine established on a single verse of Scripture and especially cautious if there is a disagreement with other Scripture.

However, the truth is joyous and liberating. All Christians should be teachers and share in the reward of the liberating power of God's Word.

F. The balance.

The cover picture shows a balance with the scale tipped in favor of tradition. I hope as you have read the book the scale has swung downward with a greater weight of truth. "And ye shall know the truth, and the truth shall make you free." John 8:32.

Scriptural Index

Subject Index